music

www.thegoodwebguide.co.uk

thegoodwebguide

music

mary-louise harding

The Good Web Guide Limited • London

First Published in Great Britain in 2000 by The Good Web Guide Limited
Broadwall House, 21 Broadwall, London, SE1 9PL

www.music.thegoodwebguide.co.uk
Email:feedback@thegoodwebguide.co.uk

10 9 8 7 6 5 4 3 2 1

A catalogue record for this book is available from the British Library.

ISBN 1-903282-11-x

Managing Editor Michelle Clare
Editor Kevin Harley

Design by Myriad Creative Ltd.

Additional Design by Zoe Marshall.

Printed in Italy at LEGO S.p.A.

contents

the good web guides

The World Wide Web is a vast resource, with millions of sites on every conceivable subject. There are people who have made it their mission to surf the net: cyber-communities have grown, and people have formed relationships and even married on the net.

However, the reality for most people is that they don't have the time or inclination to surf the net for hours on end. Busy people want to use the internet for quick access to information. You don't have to spend hours on the internet looking for answers to your questions and you don't have to be an accomplished net surfer or cyber wizard to get the most out of the web. It can be a quick and useful resource if you are looking for specific information.

The Good Web Guides have been published with this in mind. To give you a head start, our researchers have looked at hundreds of sites and what you will find in the Good Web Guides is a collection of reviews of the best we've found.

The Good Web Guide recommendation is impartial, and all the sites have been visited several times. Reviews are focused on the website and what it sets out to do, rather than an endorsement of a company, or their product. A small but beautiful site run by a one-man band may be rated higher than an ambitious but flawed site run by a mighty organisation.

Relevance to the UK-based visitor is also given a high premium: tantalising as it is to read about purchases you can make in California, because of delivery charges, import duties, and controls it may not be as useful as a local site.

Our reviewers considered a number of questions when reviewing the sites, such as: How quickly do the sites and individual pages download? Can you move around the site easily and get back to where you started, and do the links work? Is the information up to date and accurate? And is the site pleasing to the eye and easy to read? More importantly, we also asked whether the site has something distinctive to offer, whether it be entertainment, inspiration, or pure information. On the basis of the answers to these questions, sites are given ratings out of five. As we aim only to include sites that we feel are of serious interest, there are very few low-rated sites.

Bear in mind that the collection of reviews you see here is just a snapshot of the sites at a particular time. The process of choosing and writing about sites is like painting the Forth Bridge: as each section appears complete, new sites are launched and others are modified. If you register at the Good Web Guide site you can check out the reviews of new sites and updates of existing ones.

As this is the first edition of the Good Web Guide, all our sites have been reviewed by the author and research team, but we would like to know what you think. Contact us via the website or email feedback@thegoodwebguide.co.uk. You are welcome to recommend sites, quibble about the ratings, point out changes and inaccuracies, or suggest new features to assess.

You can find us at: www.music.thegoodwebguide.co.uk

introduction

Whether fan, aspiring musician or industry executive, the web will revolutionise your musical life. MP3 – the most common format used to make audio possible on the Internet – is officially the most searched term online. In cyberspace, music is now bigger than sex. Like online romping, the online musical experience provides entirely new ways to explore your subject. An MP3 makes it possible for anyone with access, to instantly make music available to anyone else who has a computer connected to a phone line. Unrestricted, instant, unfettered sonic experience; where, when and however you may want it.

However, the Internet can be as frustrating as it is liberating. There are literally thousands of sites offering some kind of sonic surf experience, and it can take hours, days, even weeks repeatedly landing at duff destinations and hitting tacky dead-ends before you find somewhere worth hanging out at for a while.

Over the past year there has been something of a goldrush within the online world, with every MBA and their dog, frankly, rushing to make millions in this dramatic new emerging market, and none more so than within the music industry. Music fans have been bombarded with new companies promising that the sonic surfer's musical pot of gold lies at their site. Only a few of them deliver, and some of the most highly advertised URLS are notable by their absence.

This book contains in-depth reviews of the essential web tools to experience music audio and video content and a simple advice section on getting started.

Each chapter – from download and streaming sites to fan sites – contains a handpicked selection of sites that meet strict criteria of simplicity and quality, and fundamentally offer a new and exiting way to interact with music and artists. There are sections dedicated to audio and video content and a guide to where to seek out that rare EP, in addition to in depth reviews of the only sites to hear new emerging talent.

The Good Web Guide to Music is the ultimate cultural map, and I hope it delivers the coolest, cutting edge guide to the best music content online: from sublime MP3 mayhem to the ridiculous band bonanzas. Get ready to rock digital, baby.

Mary-Louise Harding, October 2000

Mary-Louise Harding is at the forefront of the emerging online music industry as the New Media Reporter for the industry bible Music Week. She has appeared on BBC TV and radio news as an industry authority.

Acknowledgements

*Big love and respect to all the beautiful people at Music Week –
especially the man like Ajax Scott and Mr rock himself Paul
Williams – to the gorgeous Miss B for her remarkable patience
and boundless faith, Dear Duck for showing a special kind of
love, darling Mummy for an infinite number of reasons, to
Stinkspice for inspiration and snacks, to the one and only
Christopher Harding for being a safe place, to all members of the
original Colchester Crew – you know who you are – for direction
and illumination, to Sat for believing in me (fool!), to the talented
Mr Bleasdale for knowing where it's at, to the young J for
knowing how to rock n' roll, to the stylish Miss C for Notting Hill
nights, to the minx like Bonelli for being my partner in crime, to
Carter the Unstoppable news machine for showing me respect,
and last but certainly not least, to the Good Web Guide team for
publishing this little book. Peace.*

user key

£	subscription required	**IT**	Italy
R	registration required	**JAP**	Japan
🔒	secure online ordering	**NE**	Netherlands

key to countries

AUS	Australia	**NZ**	New Zealand
BEL	Belgium	**SA**	South Africa
CAN	Canada	**SIN**	Singapore
FR	France	**SWE**	Sweden
GER	Germany	**TAI**	Taiwan
IRE	Ireland	**UK**	United Kingdom
		US	United States

getting started

Music fans and musicians alike are constantly finding new and exciting ways to exploit the potential of the World Wide Web, creating new ways of experiencing music and, indeed, to make music. The opportunities are seemingly endless – from discovering a tranche of rare live recordings of your favourite artist by chatting to other fans online, to artists in the four corners of the world being able to record together, connected by an online virtual studio.

However, your magical musical internet tour is likely to be long, arduous, and not a little frustrating, without a good guide to the basics. Worry not, the Good Web Guide team have plunged into the depths of cyberspace to bring back the best tools for that smooth sonic surf.

HARDWARE

As a document-based system, the PC-configured internet is unlikely to remain the dominant access point for interactive audio and video as we move into the broadband era. Mobile phones, TV set-top boxes and even games consoles are likely to take over as we become used to wanting full-quality interactive audio and video entertainment on demand; where, when and how we want it. But for now, or at least until 2002, much of the UK population will be using the PC for access. We have based this book on what is currently accessible to most of you. When broadband access becomes a reality, watch out for future editions of the Good Web Guide to Music, and keep checking in with our website at www.thegoodwebguide.com for the most practical, useful advice on staying connected to the beat in the 21st century.

PC system requirements: Most audio software companies recommend you have a Pentium-class computer running Windows 95/98/NT 4.0/2000 using a minimum memory of 16 MB RAM. However, Windows NT 4.0/2000 with 64 MB RAM memory capacity is recommended for maximum audio quality.

You will also need a pair of speakers. Although most modern PCs and macs have built-in speakers,if you plan on listening via your computer alone you can achieve a better stereo sound through separate speakers. It is also important to check you have a sound card in your hard drive. If not, these can be easily obtained at any good consumer electronic store online. or on the high street.

There are many ways in which you can enhance and expand your sonic surf, such as taking it away from the desktop via an MP3 portable player, or by connecting your PC to your offline stereo system.

DOS AND DON'TS – THE ESSENTIAL CHECKLIST

Do download and play with as many different types of player software as your system can cope with and you can be bothered with, to find the one that suits your needs and style best. Don't be afraid to experiment; it's fun!

Do take notice of how long an audio file will take to download. It may still work out cheaper, in the days of narrowband connections, to buy the CD than pay the eventual cost of the phonecall coupled with any download charge.

Do read all the small print about postage and packaging costs before going ahead with purchase of any physical goods. For example, some US sites ship all goods across the Atlantic, which can result in an unexpected import charge when your goods arrive in the UK. Always check for hidden costs.

Don't be strongarmed into upgrading your audio software from the free to a paid for version; the free versions are almost always as good. This is especially important if you are a beginner and need to take time experimenting with different packages before you decide which one you want.

Listening to music online is easy. All you need is an MP3 player, or music-playing software that will play MP3 files (ones that end in .mp3 or .m3u). We recommend software that is capable of playing streaming MP3 files (which plays while being delivered to your computer) as well as downloaded music files (playing them from your hard drive). Streaming files will start playing almost immediately, so you can enjoy the music before choosing to download it. However, low speed streaming is useful for sampling the music, but expect a lower quality sound, similar to that of a fairly good radio signal. For CD quality, choose high speed or download the track and play it from your hard drive later. Note that attempting to stream a high speed file over a modem connection usually results in the music starting and stopping frequently.

music

overall rating:	
★ ★ ★ ★ ★	
classification:	
MP3 decoder and encoder	
updated:	
weekly	
navigation:	
★ ★ ★ ★	
content:	
★ ★ ★ ★	
readability:	
★ ★ ★ ★	
speed:	
★ ★ ★	
US	

http://www.musicmatch.com
MusicMatch

System requirements: MHz processor or better, Windows 95/98, NT 4.0 or Windows 2000, 32 MB RAM, 30 MB hard drive space, Microsoft Internet Explorer, SVGA or higher resolution monitor, 4x CD-ROM drive, SoundBlaster compatible card, speakers, CD Writer (for creating CDs in Jukebox 5.0), video card and Microsoft's Media Player 6.4 for video.

MusicMatch is designed to play the ubiquitous MP3 format and Microsoft's Windows Media file format (increasingly used by music giants such as record label EMI). MusicMatch formed as a company in 1997 and released their first jukebox player in 1998. Since then it has been expanding its technology to produce one of the most advanced, versatile tools for digital music junkies – with tech magazine Cnet recommending that its latest version (5) be downloaded by anyone interested in digital music 'as soon as is humanly possible'.

As with most popular web audio software, MusicMatch offers a free jukebox basic audio and video player, and a more advanced version for a fee ($29 in this case). The design isn't exactly aesthetically pleasing, but what makes the player stand out in the too-cool-for-school stakes is its simple ripping and encoding features, and it comes complete with a duffer's guide.

COOL STUFF

• MusicMatch claims to be the only free software which allows you to digitise your offline music collection and record and burn CDs with music from the net – if you want to bother with such 20th century relics – complete with a pretty comprehensive step-by-step guide for beginners.

• MusicMatch is partnered with a range of progressive download sites, including Epitonic and MP3.com. You can sample guest playlists – stream or download – in the Getmusic section of the site, which is especially useful for beginners.

• A guide and links to the cream of future music accessories, including portable players and digital speaker systems for the seriously wedged.

MusicMatch has also recently released a Mac-compatible version. Check the site for details.

Cutting-edge and top-of-the-range audio technology, and even if it is probably aimed at the advanced music digerati, its beginner's guides should help you to quickly become master of your digital music destiny.

music

overall rating:	★ ★ ★ ★ ★
classification:	multi-format audio/video player
updated:	regularly
navigation:	★ ★ ★ ★ ★
content:	★ ★ ★ ★ ★
readability:	★ ★ ★ ★ ★
speed:	★ ★ ★ ★
US	

http://www.quicktime.com
QuickTime

System requirements: PC: Pentium-based PC or compatible computer, at least 16MB of RAM ,Windows 95 or later, or Windows NT 4.0 system software, a Sound Blaster or compatible sound card and speakers, direct X version 3.0 or later recommended; MAC: power-pc processor-based Macintosh with at least 16MB RAM, MAC OS 7.5.5 or later.

It is widely accepted that Apple Macintosh are at the forefront of professional creative desktop technology, and the award-winning QuickTime is no exception. First released in 1991, before many companies had even discovered the web, QuickTime quickly became the standard for the creation and delivery of multimedia content, and it is currently used with 18,000 CD-ROMs, websites and professional video editing.

In keeping with the iMac image, the site is chunky, clean and simple to navigate, and the download process for the free player is well-explained and easy to follow. Just select the download tab at the top of the homepage and follow the instructions. It may take twice as long to install once the download is complete, as with other players, but QuickTime, with its extensive editing pause and jump features for audio and video and recording features, is still for the more discerning sonic surfer.

COOL STUFF

• Like Real and Microsoft Windows Media, Apple has collated a music TV channel with easy links to various rich streaming sources such as MTV.com, unsigned music site popwire, and classical and jazz destination site Global Music Network.

• Some QuickTime configured movies and images are embedded with 'hotspots'. These trigger off info windows such as the lyrics to the song being sung or a link to places to get tickets for an artist's next show.

OTHER STUFF

The QuickTime Plug-in plays MP3, Flash, AVI and WAV files, text tracks and sprites, and even lets your Mac or PC moonlight as a karaoke machine.

A slick, professional player for the more advanced user and potential developers.

music

overall rating:
★ ★ ★ ★ ★
classification:
Audio/video player
updated:
daily
navigation:
★ ★ ★ ★ ★
content:
★ ★ ★ ★ ★
readability:
★ ★ ★ ★ ★
speed:
★ ★ ★ ★ ★
US

http://www.realaudio.com
Real Networks

System requirements: (for the basic jukebox) Windows 95 or later, or Windows NT 4.0 with Service Pack 4, Intel(r) Pentium(r) 200MHz MMX, Cyrix(r) 6x86MX PR233, or AMD(r) K5 PR-200 32MB of RAM 200MB for Music Full Duplex Sound card and speakers 16-bit color video card and CD-ROM Drive.

Real Networks, the company behind all Real Audio technology software, were the first commercial outfit to develop a means of listening to and storing MP3s via personal computers connected to the web back at the dawn of popular cyberspace consciousness in 1995. It released its jukebox for audio and video streaming, download playback and organisation in 1999, and has since released faster and better versions, culminating in its full entertainment centre software at an alarming rate.

As Real Audio is the pioneer, almost all music content (about 85 per cent) on the web is formatted to be compatible with its software, making the RealPlayer and jukebox the real must-have for the super-sonic surf. What's more, Real Audio has the most extensive network of partners, and seems to know pretty much where the online music happenings are at. You will find exclusive features on artists such as Common, through to Britney Spears, plus MP3s of the day on its Musicnet spin-off (www.realguide.real.com/musicnet).

Although the simple download process takes a little longer to get through than others, the site is easy to navigate, and it clearly indicates which systems will support each of its many products, and which are free or paid-for. And if they do tend to come across with a touch of the Big Brother, remember that you don't have to put in your personal details, or agree to them collecting information on your download/streaming habits if you don't want to.

COOL STUFF

• Being a bit longer in the tooth than most of the audio-tech brats, Real has established meaty UK and European sites. The UK site at www.europe.real.com has UK-relevant content and links, such as a summer festival archive which offers video footage of the big 2000 events – including Glastonbury and the Leeds and Berlin Love Parades – in partnership with music news and info sites such as dotmusic.

• Instant access and search facilities for online radio will find a station to match your tastes and start streaming immediately.

• This is the most versatile technology we came across for basic download, playback, and streaming. It will stream uninterrupted, smooth audio on the most basic of systems and modem connections (within reason).

• If you download the full free entertainment centre, you automatically get a Real download manager which keeps a running log of download progress in a separate window, and applies to the relevant player software to run.

Real Networks is the herald of MP3 downloading technology and is a thoroughly comprehensive outfit. The extensive contacts with the the online music world will give you massive flexibility in downloading, streaming and playback.

http://www.sonique.com

Sonique

System requirements: Pentium 100 or faster, Windows 95 onwards or NT 4.0, 16MB RAM, 16 bit colour video card, and a sound card.

Software: Quicktime, Shockwave, Flash, Rioport.

Sonique is a little hard to get the hang of, but it is one of the cooler pieces of software. It is made by aliens (according to the site) and perhaps inspired by Kai's Power Tools. If you're a techie, this little arcade game-esque player will entertain you as much as the music you listen to on it, featuring surreal colour animation that can be torn down and rebuilt like Lego.

Fusing a highly stylized aesthetic with a fluid, windowless interface and fully animated menu systems, Sonique will play your CDs as well as MP3s, WAVs and Windows Media files. There's also a full-featured playlist editor, a variety of fun add-ons, and a robust control set featuring pitch, balance and amplification adjustment, as well as a 20-band equalizer with spline-based level adjustment. If you still haven't found the player to suit your style, Sonique could be the one.

COOL STUFF

• Multi-language options and no hard-sell. Sonique's parents like to give their little player baby away in return for your loyalty.

overall rating:
★ ★ ★ ★ ★
classification:
semi-pro audio player
updated:
weekly
navigation:
★ ★ ★ ★
content:
★ ★ ★ ★
readability:
★ ★ ★ ★
speed:
★ ★ ★ ★
US

overall rating:
★ ★ ★ ★ ★
classification:
Studio pro software
updated:
weekly
navigation:
★ ★ ★ ★ ★
content:
★ ★ ★ ★
readability:
★ ★ ★ ★
speed:
★ ★ ★ ★ ★
UK

http://www.visiosonic.com
Visiosonic

System requirements: Windows 95/98, Pentium 233Mhz or Equivalent, Windows Media Player 6.4, DirectX 5.0, 16 Mb RAM, and a sound card.

This teched-out virtual wheels-of-steel piece of software, the only British-made on the list, does more than simply turn your computer into two Technics decks. It's a dream come true for bedroom DJ's – we're talking audio and video support for mixing and fading between tracks, a virtual record crate to store and organize all of your media files, and easy access to files on the internet if you're connected.

You can even create little subfolders for all your different spaced out mixes or cyberspace genres. This tripped-out pool of code also allows you to play videos full-screen or in windows associated with whatever audio file you want to play alongside it. To top it off, installing Visiosonic's PCDJ Phat Player is pure simplicity, and the site design is pure eye candy.

COOL STUFF

• Visiosonic has developed a supersonic range of software for beginner and pro-DJs. Check out the PCDJ Mixmaster kit, complete with ripper, and a range of soft and hardware kits that enable the more dedicated (and wealthy) DJs to cut-up, mix, program, and scratch.

• The software is linked to some of the UK's most cutting edge, underground independent dance labels and sites, giving you a sneaky back porthole into where it's really at.

• At www.sonicvibes.com, Visiosonic has developed its own 24/7 radio. Linked from the site, it broadcasts explosive sets across the dance spectrum, ranging from the mainstream Ministry end, to rare slots from Cold Fusion. The station also has uncensored, live and direct interviews with some of the genre's most maverick warriors.

A god-send for DJs of all standards, this software can provide links to the roots of the underground dance scene, and lets you reach the limits of mixing, scratching, fading and programming.

music

http://www.liquidaudio.com
Liquid Audio

System requirements: Windows 95, or Windows NT 4.0 with Service Pack 4, Intel Pentium 200MHz MMX, Cyrix 6x86MX PR233, or AMD(r) K5 PR-200, 32MB of RAM, 200MB for Music Full Duplex sound card and speakers 16-bit colour video card, CD-ROM Drive, and RealPlayer G2 (version 6) or later.

Liquid Audio cannot be ignored as it is, like Microsoft, increasingly being chosen by digital music providers and owners of content (labels, publishers) to format pirate-proof music for online distribution. Rightly or wrongly, Liquid is more focused on being the digital chum of choice for record labels and retailers than the consumer interface. As a result, they are very strict about free access to music; don't expect Liquid-affilliated sites and Liquid codec tracks to offer longer than 30-second sample streams. It's like going to a listening post in a store and hearing a sample rather than the full CD.

But if you decide you want to pay as much to download an album as you do to buy one in a store, downloading its player is a must. Not only is it simple to download, it also offers the basic streaming and download playback features you'll expect, and is better quality than the usual alternative in the Windows Media brochure.

The site offers easy enough navigation, even if its intrusive advertising takes up the bottom half of the page, so that you have to scroll and squint to read a single page.

COOL STUFF

• The Liquid player has simple button options, and, carried by its affilliate music network partners (which include the main high street brands such as Tower and HMV, and some of the best music etailers such as Face the Music), it offers (paid) downloads, album artwork, sleeve notes and lyrics.

• If you have a CD-ROM drive to support it, Liquid offers simple one-step CD burning, for those who find playing the groove on their computer just not sexy enough.

•The site features a link to a different music download ecommerce site each week, so it is worth checking in if you're a beginner, in order to extend your purchasing horizons.

The player is the most professional looking of the lot, with high quality graphics and a smooth paid-for service.

music

overall rating:	
★ ★ ★ ★	
classification:	
Streaming & downloading	
updated:	
daily	
navigation:	
★ ★ ★ ★	
content:	
★ ★ ★ ★	
readability:	
★ ★ ★ ★	
speed:	
★ ★ ★ ★	
US	

http://www.winamp.com
Winamp

System requirements: A fast 486 or (optimally) a Pentium or better, running Windows 95, 98, 2000, or NT 4.

Perhaps because of its bundling with AOL access packages since its developer Nullsoft was bought by the internet giant in June 1999, Winamp is almost definitely the most popular player among PC users. Along with Real Networks, Winamp remains the darling choice for thousands of MP3 mavericks and net audio samplers alike. It's easy to install, easy to use, highly configurable, and it looks pretty cool, with hundreds of skins to choose from.

Simply install and run, drag your MP3 files into the program window, and you'll be ready to rock digital. You can also set up Winamp so that it will play an MP3 file when you double click on it. Just open the program, press Ctrl-P on your keyboard, and use the set-up screen to register the .mp3 extension to Winamp. It will support all file types from MP3, to the new Windows Media format.

COOL STUFF

• Winamp's developers created the Shoutcast Network, possibly the widest radio network online, and Winamp users have direct, simple links into all Shoutcast stations. Just follow the links, which are distinguished by genre, to start streaming.

• Winamp offers its own free branded online virtual MP3 storage through a partnership with Myplay.com (see download and streaming sites), meaning that you can store even more music without clogging up your hard drive. Link and instructions are clearly labelled on the Winamp home page.

• Weekly updated free audio and exclusive special offers via legal download directory site Getmusic.com.

• A page full of fun plug-ins, ranging from DJ tools MP3jockey to Mpeg dancers which obligingly groove along your desktop to your music, while you control the lighting and, ahem, angles. Pure gimmick-geek-cool.

Winamp is the PC user's favourite choice. With easy access, slick DJ tools and connections to one of the internet's largest radio networks, it's easy to see why.

music

overall rating:
★ ★ ★

classification:
Player and recorder software

updated:
daily

navigation:
★ ★ ★ ★

content:
★ ★ ★ ★

readability:
★ ★ ★ ★

speed:
★ ★ ★ ★

US

http://www.voquette.com
Voquette

System requirements: Pentium 166 MHz processor or better, Windows 95 or NT 4.0, US Windows OS only, 32 MB RAM, 30 MB hard drive space; Sound card and speakers, Internet Explorer 3.X, Netscape Navigator 3.X.

Software: Microsoft's Media Player, Real Networks' Real Player

If you want digital music on demand wherever you are, it is worth looking at Voquette's shiny new Media Manager 1.4. This compact software player's unique text-to-speech technology allows you to download, transfer, and listen to MP3s, audio streams, text documents, and e-mail. You can easily transfer your awaiting audio to MP3 players, Netrecorders, and Minidisc players.

Voquette's new Media Manager also allows you to organise Web-based audio, including Real, MP3, Windows Media format and others. Then, at the touch of a button, you can record that audio onto your cassette player or minidisc, or burn it onto an old CD. Finally, Voquette offers support for play lists and a personal Voquette page on their site. The downside is that, although the player is free, to get to all the cool bits, like transferring files to the car, you should be prepared to part with some cash. Otherwise, being totally reliable, almost totally idiot-proof, and full of features, the NetLink has us jazzed.

COOL STUFF

• Play and record unrestricted formats, such as WAV, MP3 and WMA.

• It edits out net congestion and buffering breaks automatically.

• You can record and save live shows and radio broadcast direct to your netman via Voquette, as well as straight audio files.

• Will manage daily subscriptions to must-have content on a daily basis.

Voquette's hot skill is the smooth translation of text into sound, allowing you to download and transfer emails, MP3s audio streams and text messages, and listen to them wherever you are.

music

overall rating:
★ ★ ★
classification:
Audio/video player software
updated:
daily
navigation:
★ ★ ★ ★
content:
★ ★ ★ ★
readability:
★ ★ ★ ★
speed:
★ ★ ★ ★
US

http://www.windowsmedia.com
WindowsMedia

System requirements: Intel Pentium II 266 MHz or better, 64 MB RAM or greater, Windows 98 or Windows NT Server version 4.0 with SP4.

The controversial Dark Lord of Cyberspace is gradually beginning to dominate entertainment technology, closing in on early rising stars Real Networks and Winamp. Like or loathe Bill Gates, you can't deny that he's good at the software game. What's more, even if Microsoft's music content recommendations are not exactly cutting-edge, he is rapidly using its powerful position to offer some of the best multimedia content online.

As ageing plastic manufacturers (traditionally known as major record labels) and high street music retailers dip their toes into the download and streaming blackhole, Microsoft's streaming windows media technology is increasingly becoming the preferred choice, making it hard to avoid for legal music content.

The Windows Media Player (version 6.4 for Windows 95 and the latest version 7 for Windows 98 and NT, and a Mac version) can be downloaded in two simple steps in about 20 minutes from the Microsoft.com site. Once it is downloaded, you are directed towards www.windowsmedia.com for recommended content.

COOL STUFF

• You can hide the corporate parents-choice standard look player with a larger than usual choice of skins. Make your player look like a lump of goo or an alien. Only available for version 7, however.

Microsoft's reliable and super-power identity has attracted the middle-of-the-road users who want to play it safe. The obvious choice for legal downloading.

music

OTHER SITES OF INTEREST

Macromedia
http://www.macromedia.com
Many of the best music sites, especially zines and artist sites, use Macromedia Flash and Shockwave animation. We strongly recommend you take the time to visit this site to get the free, quickly downloaded plug-ins to transform your surf. Simply click on the download button at the top of the homepage and follow the instructions to download both at the same time. Once they have been downloaded you will receive an email telling you all about the content, aggregated at www.shockwave.com. This site is worth a visit, especially for an easy, step-by-step introduction to what the web can be with animation. You can also opt for the free Shockmachine video/audio player download. (See full review of content in download and streaming chapter.)

PlayJ
http://www.playj.com
This site invites you, rather predictably, to join the new music revolution by either downloading its player or downloading a plug-in compatible with the Winamp or Media Player software. PlayJ is slightly different to most other player software providers, in that its parent company, EverAd Inc, has developed its own file codec .plj, and claims to have secured deals with over 70 independent labels to distribute their music in this

format. The site has a useful search engine for PlayJ affilliated artists, and useful genre pages with info and downloads. The player also accepts MP3 files, but does not support streaming.

RadioDestiny Network
http://www.radiodestiny.com
The destiny media player is a cheeky little MP3 player, as well as an excellent front-end to the many internet broadcasting stations available on the RadioDestiny Network. One of the web's best-kept secrets, the site packs the usual features but with superior links to some of the best independent broadcasts on the web.

FreeAmp
http://www.freeamp.org
This cross-platform audio player features an optimised version of the GPLed Xing MPEG decoder which makes it one of the fastest and best sounding players available. FreeAmp provides a number of the most common features that you will come to expect in a clean, easy-to-use interface.

Namezero.com
http://www.k-jofol.org
If you're a true techie web noise junky, k-jöfol will be your nirvana. Just step up and drool over the quickest decoding engine and some of the sharpest sounds and funkiest interface in the internet world.

music

MP3 World

http://www.mp3-world.com

A familiar explorer interface makes for super-simple navigation of this playlist editor programme. For when your digital music collection needs a filing assistant.

CyberTropix

http://www.cybertropix.com

Describing itself as the last of the independent digital audio sites, CyberTropix is a fantastic resource, if unimaginatively designed, for up-to-date reviews and links to almost any MP3 player, management, and associated software downloads that any self-respecting MP3 marauder should know about.

Section 02

directories, portals & ezines

The internet is absolutely stuffed with sites attempting to be the definitive portal or destination site for all aspects of popular music. Unsurprisingly, a great many of them are ugly, misinformed, out of date and basically a waste of surf time. This chapter reviews the best portals, destination sites, music news and information stations along with ezines designed to save the trawl and cut straight to the chase. One of the most fundamental criteria for a Good Web Guide To Music site inclusion is its unique functionality. The internet is a new medium and can be used to solve information, communication and access problems that dead trees, dog'n bone and terrestrial TV could never have dreamt of attempting. If it ain't doing anything new or innovative online – especially if its an established old media brand – it's not going in. Welcome to where it's at for music windows, search engines, news, reviews features and links.

music

overall rating:
★ ★ ★ ★ ★

classification:
electronic music search engine

updated:
weekly

navigation:
★ ★ ★ ★ ★

content:
★ ★ ★ ★

readability:
★ ★ ★ ★

speed:
★ ★ ★ ★ ★

US

http://www.beatseek.com
Beatseek

Don't be fooled by this site's plain design. It's not built for visual titilation, but as a comprehensive portal to everything related to electronic music online. Beatseek probably ranks with the best household name portals in providing an exhaustive window to the web for this genre, which it describes as including, house, trance, ambient, drum'n'bass, techno and more.

You can choose to search its database from a particular reference point on the search page – say, Aphex Twin – or choose the directory page and follow the links to the category that best fits your line of inquiry. The site also collates relevant news headlines which you can search, or browse, from the likes of Radio One and ClubPlanet.com (see p.63). Incredibly simple to navigate, Beatseek is possibly the best launch pad for online electronica you're likely to find.

COOL STUFF

• Exhaustive hyperlink news headlines from around the web, bringing you a daily update of all that's making the news from the world of electronic music.

• A daily email subscription will deliver a précis of news, new site features, and recently added recommended sites direct to your inbox. Simply submit your address in the relevant window on the homepage.

• The broadcast channel allows you to search the web for broadcasts which bring you the beats you want to hear 24/7.

• The Forums Search lists all discussions and chatrooms going on around the web by specific category or broad genre within the electronic music sector.

A fantastic portal resource (especially suitable for sonicweb newbies) for finding webcasts, forums and sites related to electronic music.

music

overall rating:	★★★★★
classification:	UK indie/alternative
updated:	daily
navigation:	★★★★★
content:	★★★★
readability:	★★★★
speed:	★★★★★
UK	

http://www.channelfly.com

channelfly

Software: Real Player, Liquid, QuickTime or Windows Media Player

Since its launch late last year, London alternative promoters and magazine publishers Barfly have turned this site into a sophisticated, multimedia-rich news and web-event music site. Given its unique access to one of central London's busiest alternative gig venues, channelfly's live interview and music webcasts with the UK indie scene's brightest rising stars (such as Coldplay and Badly Drawn Boy) are unrivalled in consistency and quality.

The site design is Flash-rich but clean, sexy, sophisticated, and simple to navigate. The five channels – news, aboutmusic, reviews, MP3s and webcast, live music and user area – are each listed across the top of the homepage and divided into subsections which you can pick via drop-down menus when rolling the mouse across the channel logos. Nice.

COOL STUFF

• The MP3 and webcast channel is the best feature of this site, with all archived webcasts listed by artist, and a highlighted graphic hyperlink depicting which format each show is in.

• The live and single/album reviews here are best-of-breed.

• Get a comprehensive guide to immediately upcoming gigs at the Barfly or its extensive nationwide partner venues, such as Sheffield's Leadmill and Dingwalls in Camden Town. There is, however, no method of online ticket booking or phone details.

OTHER STUFF

Subscribe to channelfly email updates, offers, and the Fly magazine by filling in your details in the user area section.

The competitions section of the News & Stuff channel offers you the chance to win prizes, ranging from a hot air balloon ride across London, to t-shirts and CDs in several competitions.

The extensive news and features section offers offbeat news from the world of indie rock, along with stylishly written and presented features on up-and-coming bands and interviews with established acts.

A sublime one-stop shop for indie fans nationwide.

music

overall rating:
★ ★ ★ ★ ★

classification:
UK drum 'n' bass specialist

updated:
weekly

navigation:
★ ★ ★ ★ ★

content:
★ ★ ★ ★

readability:
★ ★ ★ ★

speed:
★ ★ ★ ★ ★

UK

http://www.breakbeat.co.uk
Drum & Bass Arena

Software: Flash, Real, Microsoft Windows Media and Liquid Audio players.

Despite the URL, this long-standing, award-winning site is actually known and referred to as the Drum & Bass Arena. Like hip-hop, drum'n'bass is well represented on the web, as you'll see in the artists, fanclubs and label sites chapter. However, Drum & Bass Arena is the only site that manages to straddle the mélange of styles and influences within the UK (and to a lesser extent the US scenes) to produce a compelling and vibrant site.

Sporting an appropriately bold, semi-industrial interface, the homepage is packed full of links to special features, DJ interviews and streams, reviews of recent parties and latest news from what continues to be one of the most active and progressive scenes of the UK underground. Go straight through to featured links or pick a feature listed under the five main channel headings – records, specials, interact, DJs and MCs – on the left-hand side. This site is the ultimate catch-all cyber destination for any self-respecting drum'n'bass head.

COOL STUFF

• The Arena features new live DJ mix streams of excellent quality, and live party webcasts each week, and you'll find all recent streams archived for playback via Windows Media Player in the

Listen section of the Records channel. Also in the superb Listen channel, catch samples of selected tracks from all major album and single releases. All releases are listed with play, review, and comment links, and some are available for purchase by clicking on the buy button to take you into a separate window of UK ecommerce partner WHSmith's cdparadise.com. Original early 1990s fans who've had their tapes and vinyl disappear can take a trip back to their hardcore junglist massive daze in the classics section of the Listen channel, with full streams of over 50 tracks available.

• Seek out that rare vinyl or sell some of your old records via the want in the Records channel. You can read through the postings, or post your own message in the form provided on the page, or search cdparadise.

• Purchase a selection of singles via Liquid Audio secure digital download on the Digital Downloads page. You need the free Liquid Audio player installed first.

OTHER STUFF

• View current and archived world top ten drum'n'bass tracks and artists' current top five picks in the the records channel.

• Vent your spleen on the scene rant of the month on the hot topic page in the Specials channel.

• Vote on the topic of the month – such as your favourite UK drum'n'bass MC – on the Polls page.

• Watch streaming video interviews with top UK drum'n'bass DJs and producers on the Interviews page.

• Check out which DJs are rocking the scenes in the top venues around the world – from Hawaii to Estonia to Brazil – on the World Scenes page.

• Join the worldwide general or producers email mailing lists, email a drum'n'bass question to the Arena crew in the Interactive channel, or join the newsgroup or chatroom to get views on latest releases and tips on upcoming events.

• Listen to MC samples or full rhymes from both established and up and coming MC's in the DJ/MCs channel.

A comprehensive and rich source of audio and all the latest news and views from the vibrant underground UK D&B scene, with dispatches from around the world.

http://www.gopophits.com

gopophits

Software: Real player

After hours of trawling around the web seeking out the funkiest music pages for your delectation, gopophits really is a site for sore eyes. Fantastically decked out in kitsch, spangly star wrap wallpaper, with splodges of TOTP circa 1974-style channel links, this site is perfect for teen girlies hungry for popstar news, gossip, competitions and online chat. Drag the stars around the homepage or delve into each of the four channels to write a letter on the topic of the day or chat with pop fans around the world. More than anything, just enjoy online poparama in rare advertisement-free style, delivered with pizzazz.

COOL STUFF

• Kill all four aliens on the gossip page with the sliding space gun to get each tasty bit of Britpop Chinese whispers.

• Be an agony aunt to angst-ridden teen pop stars in the Pop Head Shop section of the stories channel. Click on the link and a window pops up with a real audio clip of the star of the week explaining their personal dilemma, to which you can respond with advice in the box next to the pic. Too cool for school.

• Send in pictures and stories about your popstar lookalike, bedroom poster shrine, or photo or story about a star to be posted in the You Are The Star section of the club channel.

overall rating:	
★★★★★	
classification:	
teen pop community	
updated:	
daily	
navigation:	
★★★★★	
content:	
★★★★	
readability:	
★★★★	
speed:	
★★★★★	
UK	

• Chat with teen popsters from around the world in the chat pop-up window.

OTHER STUFF

• In the club channel, you can rate the week's pop releases in the reviews section, post your rants on what really bugs you about popdom, post funny pop stories in the letters section, and test your teen-pop knowledge in the quiz section.

• Vote on a serious weekly news topic. For example, should pop stars stop snogging each other in public and stick to singing?!

A fun, heavily interactive, super-stylish and non-patronising site, perfect for young teen-pop obsessives.

http://www.hookt.com
Hookt

Software: Flash & Macromedia, Real player

Hookt is a New York-based collective bringing a fresh slice of funky and lively hip-hop action to the web with masterful style. Flash-heavy and shot through with soulful breaks, the site can take a little longer than some to download with slower speed connections. But it is worth it. The web might be slammed with different crews trying to represent the true flava, but this has to be one of the best sites available.

After a simple Flash intro with spinning decks, you can choose from clicking on the features which scroll through the central animated graphic equalizer or the graphic channel links across the top, which shout their names as you slide the mouse across and display a sub-menu of choices on the left of the screen.

With each channel accompanied by its own fresh beat loop and supa-phat graphics, Hookt is keeping it real in true style.

COOL STUFF

• Pick up previously unreleased MP3s from the likes of Snoop Dogg and Lil' Kim in Jackin' for Treats, watch free stream videos in See what I'm Sayin, stream the top five picks of the week in Top Billin', read the crew's reviews and listen again in Ill Analysis, listen to streams from the likes of the Wu-Tung Clan in

overall rating:	
★ ★ ★ ★ ★	
classification:	
hip-hop music and style	
updated:	
daily	
navigation:	
★ ★ ★ ★ ★	
content:	
★ ★ ★ ★	
readability:	
★ ★ ★ ★	
speed:	
★ ★ ★ ★ ★	
US	

the sound archive, and read or listen and watch interviews with the East Coast's finest in Headlinerz. There are also style gurus in All Pointz Bulletin and label headz in Big Dogs. In the Soundz channel, you can also test your rhyming MC skills and do battle with some serious lyricists on the Battle Boardz.

• If you've fancied playing with samples and creating your own loops, check out the Beat Bomb channel, making sure you have Macromedia shockwave installed first.

• The Tagline channel gives you the chance to leave your mark on the NY subway without getting chased. Pick a section and colour and spray your name.

OTHER STUFF

• Check out what threadz are down in NY in the Wearz channel.

• Get the latest East Coast happenings in the news channel.

Breakbeat through and through, and chocca with bad-ass attitude, this is the site for hip-hop junkies.

http://www.sonicnet.com

Sonicnet

Software: Windows Media Player for radio content.

Award-winning music-news-focused site Sonicnet should be on every online music explorer's hit list for its excellent general pop news coverage. The bias is towards the US, currently, and they probably need a UK-based team to cover offline music events in Blighty. That may change soon, however, with the rather delayed launch of a UK site by Sonicnet sister MTV.

MTV's parent Viacom has so far launched an online version of broadcast music video channel VH1 (www.VH1-online.co.uk) and, as mentioned, an MTV UK site (www.mtv.co.uk), and has Swiss, German and Japanese Sonicnet sites. However, for the purpose of the Good Web Guide, we still feel that sonicnet.com is the brightest child, with other members of the family still little more than online promotional plugs for its broadcast output.

Sonicnet stands out from the crowd for its award-winning news coverage and its breadth and depth of genre coverage. One simple click on a genre from the clearly labelled homepage will take you to news, a promotional download of the day or the relevant Sonicnetradio channel. Choose from Pop, Jazz, Classical, Rock, World/International, Dance/Electronic, R&B/Soul, Hip-Hop/Rap, Blues/Folk or country. One of the few streaming options configured for low bandwidth dial-up connections, Sonicnet is king of the audio surf!

overall rating:	★★★★★
classification:	mainstream news and reviews
updated:	daily
navigation:	★★★★★
content:	★★★★
readability:	★★★★
speed:	★★★★★
US	

COOL STUFF

• Register and receive a weekly email updating on the latest hot news and juicy gossip, current download offers and ways to win some pretty cool prizes. Receive headlines across the board or configure to your genre tastes, or choose to receive Sonicnet's excellent coverage from the digital frontline.

• Often gets online exclusives – the first (legal) showing of Madonna's video, for example – due to the bargaining power of its offline sisters, MTV and VH1.

• Sonicnet hosts daily live streaming video and webchat 'events' – find the schedules and an idiot's guide to taking part in the events channel. Log-on, drop-out.

• Find biographies, discographies, reviews, news, audio, videos, concerts and links for your favourite artists via the super sonicnet all-music directory channel. Search results will offer a customised email on tour dates, new releases and other relevant info for that artist, as well as suggest a Sonicnet radio channel playing your favoured artist.

A broad news and interactive event led mainstream music site with exhaustive attention to detail and an unmistakable raison d'être.

http://www.yahoo.com

Yahoo!

A web portal veteran, Yahoo! knows how to scour the web and serve up a tasty slice of general music activity online. Its main strengths are aggregation of news from various sources such as Rollingstone.com and Sonicnet and an industrial strength directory search – of course, Yahoo!'s original core business.

If you've got time on your hands and contacts to make, the breadth and reach of Yahoo!'s music message boards and chat rooms are rarely rivalled on the web, and are clearly linked on the left-hand column of the homepage. However, the search functions on this site really are king, with categories ranging from labels to specialist genres. If you've got a thirst for all the knowledge available on the web about your pet music subject, be it Japanese hardcore teen rock or Captain Beefheart, Yahoo! will usually have the answer.

overall rating:
★ ★ ★ ★ ★

classification:
mainstream news and reviews

updated:
daily

navigation:
★ ★ ★ ★ ★

content:
★ ★ ★ ★

readability:
★ ★ ★ ★

speed:
★ ★ ★ ★ ★

US

COOL STUFF

• Yahoo! has put together its very own branded audio/video player software, capable of playing all known file formats, complete with a useful 'Digital Browser' function. This enables you to hear news, downloads and video/chat events linked on the Yahoo music homepage, as well as to add your own choices to a favourites feature, as you would with your general internet browser. The player also contains a search function within it, allowing you to scour the web for audio files for, say, Aphex

Twin, and store them in your playlist. An exhaustive idiot's guide on how to use all of this comes in handy too!

A wealthy window to the world of music online, suitable for newbies or anoraks seeking out that hard-to-find official Sabrina fan page, or something.

http://www.angrycoffee.com
Angry Coffee

Angry Coffee is a fantastic resource for audio online, especially for beginners. Launched by a set of seasoned Bay area net musicians in summer 1999, the site recently hit the headlines for its Napster-like feature, Perculator, which allows you to search the systems of a number of free MP3 file sharing sites, including Napster, for that controversial free sonic hit.

However, it is uncertain how long this feature will stick around on the site, once the US record labels association the RIAA get their teeth into it. The good news there is that Angry Coffee is more than an MP3 file sharing resource. Its MP3, Flash, Beatnik and QuickTime software step-by-step interactive tutorials are second to none – you won't find a better way to get started.

The design is bold, with each channel clearly linked on the right and left of the homepage. Aside from the wicked tutorials, it carries weekly musings from music and internet thinkers pondering the impact of Generation Y, technology and progressive artists on the established label-based music industry. It has fantastic links to reliable news sources and online radio stations, too.

COOL STUFF

• At the top of the homepage, Perculator invites you to search an artist or song title, like you would a subject in a regular search

overall rating:	★ ★ ★ ★
classification:	tutorial, download, streaming
updated:	daily
navigation:	★ ★ ★ ★ ★
content:	★ ★ ★ ★
readability:	★ ★ ★ ★
speed:	★ ★ ★ ★ ★
US	

engine, and serves up a list of brews for your delectation before you can say: 'my god, they ripped off Napster!' Each track listing shows the size of the file and the speed of connection of the person serving it. Select a track or 10 and begin pouring the heady stuff onto your hardrive.

• The site invites unsigned artists to send in their work to be hosted on the site, with artists' separate pages within the Angry Coffee frame, for a $10 fee. Unlike some sites which solicit unsigned material, Angry Coffee won't demand the rights, digital or otherwise, to artists' songs. Different artists are featured as a main item on the homepage each week, with links to their site, plus artists are recommended on the basis of users' expressed tastes. That said, Bay area artists tend to be over-represented – send over some UK Garage!

OTHER STUFF

• The Fresh Ears channel offers weekly new media music comment in Audiofile, an artist feature and a cute little animation on the Bulker page.

• Free weekly updates of new content on the site to subscribers.

A solid launch pad for online music newbies and a useful and reliable altenative to Napster (for now).

http://www.dotmusic.com

dotmusic

Software: Windows Media Player or Realplayer to see webcasts

Billing itself as 'the insider's guide to music', dotmusic is certainly the old kid on the block in the UK pop music online scene. Originally the online presence of music industry bible Music Week, dotmusic has transformed itself in recent years into a big-budget, all-singing, all-digital music network. Designed to net the young and affluent Gen Y kids and their older siblings, it offers a generous slice of what's happening in the UK's mainstream pop music scene, from news and webcasts to current chart listings and a shop powered by the pan-European entertainment etailer, Boxman. Backed by media giant United News & Media, dotmusic is likely to be a consistent, reliable and commercial online music source for years to come.

The site sports a clean, simple-to-navigate design, with the channel links constantly framed to the right of the page for quick access. If UK chart-orientated daily news, gossip and video moves your mouse, then dotmusic should suit you. It's especially useful and trustworthy for netmusic virgins.

overall rating:
★ ★ ★ ★
classification:
general pop infotainment site
updated:
daily
navigation:
★ ★ ★ ★ ★
content:
★ ★ ★ ★
readability:
★ ★ ★ ★
speed:
★ ★ ★ ★ ★
UK

COOL STUFF

• Dotmusic's search engine will update you on reviews, news and happenings as their take on the world of pop for the last six years is all archived. Search by artist, event or key word – 'Priory' for example!

• With house, trance, garage and techno genres winning great chunks of mainstream appeal, dance music is the only genre to get its separate channel on dotmusic. This summer the channel homes in on the ubiquitous Ibiza scene with an A-Z kit of events and resorts, a guide to the art of chilling, and top ten records from DJs and from record stores. Don't say Ayia or Nappa, though: the so-called new Ibiza has failed to hit dotmusic consciousness just yet. You'll also find a weekly dance news email, live and record reviews, Pete Tong and Giles Peterson's weekly Radio 1 playlists, archived vinyl recommendations from a range of DJs from Billy Nasty to Hyper, and dance label profiles in dotmusic's dance channel.

• If you want to get something off your chest about Posh Spice's tendency to mime or Eminem's tussles with the law, dotmusic's message boards in its Community Channel are usually well-populated and moderated. Some contributors centre on sex and slur, despite warnings from the dotmusic team before entering, but that's strictly for the very bored and lonely.

OTHER STUFF

• The UK's top 75 singles and albums official charts are posted on the charts channel of the site every Sunday – with clear and simple buttons to click through to dotmusic's review, a real audio clip and the shop section of the site next to each track listing.

• The charts channel has pages listing the Top 20 singles for 2000 so far, top 20 singles and albums listings for Indie Singles, Dance, UK Club, Music Videos, Jazz & Blues, R'n'B, Rock, Country and Compilations – with accompanying reviews, clips and options to buy. Nothing as controversial as full free streams, though.

• The artist channel is updated weekly with exclusive text and webcast interviews with relevant popsters doing the promotional rounds with new releases or tours. Reviews, discographies, biographies and news on the top 20 best-selling single artists is updated weekly with each new chart, and an A-Z star list gives links to official sites of all artists that have appeared on dotmusic – think more Lolly and Craig David than Derrik May or Badly Drawn Boy.

A comprehensive UK mainstream chart-based site, suitable for the casual music fan and an especially useful destination for musicnet virgins.

music

overall rating:	
★ ★ ★ ★	
classification:	
UK dance lifestyle site	
updated:	
weekly	
navigation:	
★ ★ ★ ★ ★	
content:	
★ ★ ★ ★	
readability:	
★ ★ ★ ★	
speed:	
★ ★ ★ ★ ★	
UK	

http://www.ministryofsound.com
Ministry of Sound

Software: Flash, Real and Microsoft Windows Media players

Since débuting on the internet in 1996, the commercial trance/techno/house behemoth of the British dance music movement has built up an impressive dance lifestyle site, covering festivals, Ibiza, tunes, reviews and where it thinks it's at across nine channels.

The homepage interface is pleasing to the eye and offers clear navigation links. Simply jump into Music, Clubs or Lifestyle channels from the links across the top of the page or jump to specific topics via the picture links in the main body of the page. Each channel is cleanly presented and clearly details what to expect, and, owing to the Ministry's fortunate position of hosting live dance events every week, the site is rich in audio/visual content. The only slight irritant is that MoS runs on heavy advertising revenue. The banners aren't intrusive on the pages, but you do have to put up with a pop-up window advertisement every time you click into a different section of the site.

COOL STUFF

• Tune into a cross-section of sounds via archived webcasts of the Ministry's various nights, from hard trance to old skool house and beats'n'breaks from its Logical Progression night.

• You can link to DJs' own sites and buy tracks from the radio channel in the Music section, which also offers a hefty serving of interviews, webcasts, and Ministry TV interviews and performances with DJs from popular UK house, garage, trance and techno.

• Download a wide cross-section of new and older releases from the downloads channel in the Music section. To complete the download you must have Rioport's free audio manager installed, and the download file access will expire after 30 days.

• Full audio/visual coverage of the British dance colony Ibiza in the Clubs channel, from a beginner's guide and an interactive map of the island to bi-weekly missives of the latest tunes. Plus a glance at the burgeoning Ayia Napa scene.

OTHER STUFF

• Read and watch interviews and performances with up-and-coming DJs from around the world in the DJ section, plus the latest DJ news in Informer. Also find out what MoS and its disciples rate as the top ten DJ mixes of the month and pre-release club tracks in the MoS Recommends section.

• Catch all the major clubs reviewed, Webcasts from MoS events at home and abroad and tell all about your lost weekend or look for a date on the broad, fairly well populated message boards in the Clubs channel. Plus full listings for the coming month for all the UK superclubs.

• Look up holiday bargains, through the MoS partnership with Lastminute.com, and win games and stuff on the essentials page of the Lifestyle channel.

• No self-respecting UK music vortal would be complete without its own take on the summer festivals. Find webcasts, reviews, listings and competitions in the Lifestyle channel.

A professional, clean and fun site delivering everything you would expect from UK dance's corporate mammoth, with a little bit extra on top. An impressive showing, then, from the overlords of the UK commercial dance scene.

http://www.music365.com
Music365

Launched in late 1998 as part of the well-respected 365 network of consumer interest sites, Music365 caters for the slightly older, male-rock take on news, reviews and features from the world of the UK music mainstream. Its news coverage is broad and touches all the expected bases (Napster, Robbie, Madonna at time of writing), as does its reviews and live coverage – fed through from Live!365.com.

However, as it is designed more for the football twenty to thirtysomething fanatic popping in from the hugely successful sister site Football365 for a quick update on what's hot in the world of chart music, don't expect groundbreaking exclusives on the news front. Rather, Music365 is about keeping its loyal network subscribers (Fred Zeppelin and Davey Beer Drinker) informed, up-to-date, and well-stocked with the latest CDs; you can purchase CD albums and DVDs through the site's partnership with ecommerce site Boxman, or choose your own compilation CDs through its partnership with custom CD site Cductive via its shopping channel.

The community channel promises hassle-free entry to the site's chatrooms, but we discovered that, if your browser doesn't support computer language Java, you're not going in. Otherwise, Music365 is quick and easy to navigate. Its nine channels – including community and competitions pages – are clearly labelled at the top of the homepage, along with a quick

overall rating:
★ ★ ★ ★
classification:
mainstream rock and pop
updated:
daily
navigation:
★ ★ ★ ★ ★
content:
★ ★ ★ ★
readability:
★ ★ ★ ★
speed:
★ ★ ★ ★ ★
UK

access search engine if you're after something specific. On the whole, it's not unpleasant on the eye either. Think Sky rather than NME.

COOL STUFF

• Music365's coverage of festivals and gigs in its Live channel is comprehensive and impressive. Expect reviews from all major rock/pop gigs in the UK and some from UK bands' tours in further flung territories, plus token coverage of the tipped up-and-coming rock acts too. Its Festival 2000 listings for the Northern hemisphere in its festival channel is not a bad first stop for comprehensive listings either.

• Find daily picks of new release videos – available as Real downloads from the site – and archived audio interviews and videos.

No-nonsense, honest and interactive pop/rock coverage for the 25-35 roll-with-it football shirt wearing Britman masses.

http://www.musicstation.com
Musicstation

overall rating:
★ ★ ★ ★
classification:
global music network
updated:
daily
navigation:
★ ★ ★ ★
content:
★ ★ ★ ★
readability:
★ ★ ★ ★
speed:
★ ★ ★ ★
US

Musicstation is the frontpage for three MTVi owned sites, namely Musicnewswire, Rockontv and CD-clubs. However, we recommend this site just for its musicnewswire channel. Don't bother with rockontv unless you're planning a trip to the US to watch TV for two weeks; it's just schedules of artist appearances and music programming on US channels, and CD-club is for the US mail-order CD company Columbia House. Musicnewswire aggregates the top daily news, features and reviews from a wide mix of sources including NME.com and Qonline.co.uk, sonicnet, Radio 1, Music365 and Billboard.

This is an excellent site for an overview of pan-industry major happenings, from stars' high court spats to reviews of upcoming big releases on both sides of the Atlantic. Either scroll through the headline hyperlinks of the top stories and reviews in each section – of which each source is clearly labelled – or use the instant access dropdown menu at the top to access a full list of story, review or feature links from each source. Each link will open a separate window to take you to the exact page on the source's web page for that news story, review or feature. If you haven't got the time or patience to trawl through a number of mainstream music news sources online, musicnewswire is a good time-saving device. Think utility over entertainment.

A functional site for that at-a-glance update on music headlines from a wide variety of UK and US sources.

music

overall rating:	
★ ★ ★ ★	
classification:	
multilingual music/style ezine	
updated:	
weekly	
navigation:	
★ ★ ★ ★	
content:	
★ ★ ★ ★	
readability:	
★ ★ ★ ★	
speed:	
★ ★ ★	
BEL	

http://www.nirvanet.com

Nirvanet

Software: Flash, Realplayer

Describing itself as the global network for local nomads, this site looks, at first glance, like another half-baked attempt by some well-meaning but ultimately talentless and pretentious individuals to get clever with new media. Far from it. Nirvanet is a superbly designed, intensely rich information, music and links resource for intelligent audio gratification and community.

Because of the breadth and volume of content on the site, there are several ways of getting to the information and you can get a bit lost. We recommend you close the window which automatically pops up with what's new on the site, follow the link to issue two to the left of the constellation, and then use the Access, Understand and Act pop-up menus across the bottom of the page. From virtual fantastic sonic/visual tours of Brazil to Paris in the Voyages channel, to live DJ mixes from Tokyo, to animated discourse on global warming, this site manages to weave music/culture and art to create a beautiful and unpretentious international interface for the electronic digital community.

COOL STUFF

• Click into the Voyage channel and experience some really innovative and beautiful use of sound and images. The voyage project is intended to take you on a virtual journey to the most beautiful cities on earth, reconfigured to its interpretation with sound and image selection and manipulation. Beauty, imagination and skill on this scale are rare online. Find Voyage in the Access pop-up menu at the bottom of the page.

• Visit the Soundscan channel for reviews and download links to the cream of the Web's virtual studio software for cutting and sampling. And some fun games too.

• Innovative music-making competitions, judged by the real live signed DJs. In conjunction with online music mixing software site Gizmoland.com, promised prizes include a chance to showcase music at industry events in France.

• Streamed hour-long DJ mixes, from underground DJs from Tokyo to Timbuctoo.

• Contribute to Nirvanet's thesis on images of Spain by sending in party photos and music.

• Nirvanet has its own selective search engine for like-minded sites, newsgroups and software.

OTHER STUFF

• In the Soundscan section, select the funky suprasonic pop-up channel to listen to samples and view well-reproduced artist art.

music

The Hacktive channel carries regularly updated pictures and comment on the issues surrounding music, freedom of speech, governments and emerging technology.

• Crashlab is the latest spot opened on a web network by Crashed magazine to honour French house and techno – link from the Understand menu.

• Moving away from music, if you fancy a slice of social consciousness with your daily sonic surf, check out Nirvanet's superbly presented essays on everything from Integration and Conflict in Contemporary Europe and the Space-Time Continuum, complete with sleek and effective Flash animation. You'll find these in the Understand channel.

The shop's buy links appear to be broken (better get off to Beatseek.com) but, otherwise, this is an intelligent European network linking imagination, design, music and leftfield culture to create a wonderfully sublime and rich resource.

http://www.takeoutmusic.com

Takeoutmusic

Software: Macromedia Flash plug-in, Windows Media Player, Liquid Player.

Takeoutmusic.com had to be included, if only for its the wicked Flash intro, with its funky Japanese cartoon characters and natty rhyme: 'Takeoutmusic.com... blow up the internet/competitors aren't ready yet/the future of independent music, music.....' This news, reviews and download site is aimed at street-literate youth, with an emphasis on rap and hip-hop related content.

The homepage is divided into four sections comprising news headlines and links to the news pages, plus headlines from alternative ezines Mired and Mezzmusic, competition/giveaway hyperlink headlines, similar feature headlines and featured new releases. Yet there are two other methods of navigating the site: follow the HipHop, Dance, Electronic or Rock links across the top of the homepage, or select from a complete list of channels through the bottom frame.

COOL STUFF

• Takeoutmusic has recently launched www.takeoutpop.com, a sister site to pick up fans of R&B, pop and more mainstream rock, with its own news, features, message boards and weekly email. Pink and blue pastel design and chatrooms called teentalk may be a bit too patronising for some.

overall rating:	
★ ★ ★ ★	
classification:	
street-style news and reviews	
updated:	
daily	
navigation:	
★ ★ ★	
content:	
★ ★ ★ ★	
readability:	
★ ★ ★ ★	
speed:	
★ ★ ★	
US	

• The takeoutRadio button launches you from the homepage into an eight channel streaming radio selection from Indie to Urban – easily done if you have the Windows Media Player downloaded. Click through to the takeout store to buy any track.

OTHER FEATURES

• Buy Liquid downloads or CDs, magazines and other music merchandise from the takeout store at US prices. However, don't be fooled by the books, comics, games and toys channels labelled in the store – they don't appear to be live yet. And allow a little longer for physical delivery of goods outside of the US.

• The site's loops and samples channels promises it has some of the hardest to find song snatches, for sale from contributing DJs.

• Takeoutmusic obviously don't do community too well. Despite an impressive range of eight genre boards, we spied one post.

This site is one of the trickiest in terms of navigation – and the scroll frames within the pages can be annoying – but its busy, colourful design no doubt appeals to the youth market.

http://www.webnoize.com

Webnoize

Out of the proliferating number of sites covering the emerging new media entertainment industry, Webnoize, launched in 1996, stands head and shoulders above the throng. Its emphasis is on intelligent, objective and well-informed analysis of the companies, individuals and concepts at the forefront of the digital entertainment phenomenon, rather than competing for the scoop. Many online music fans have become politicised and involved in the birth pains of burgeoning methods of access to music online due to the high-profile disputes, such as the RIAA vs MP3.com and Napster debates, between new companies meeting consumer demand for access to digital music and established music copyright owners. Webnoize is an excellent source for those who want to keep up to speed with cool new sites and ways of getting more music online, as well as for those who want to decide how to behave as an online music consumer – whether to use Napster and its like, for example.

With blue and black text set on a white, spacious background, and blue disc symbols at the top of the homepage for quick movement between channels, this site is well designed for its purpose, although it is annoyingly wide for a standard screen.

COOL STUFF

• Listen to, or watch if your connection is 56k or above, interviews and panel discussions with artists, pioneers of the

overall rating:
★ ★ ★ ★
classification:
new media news
updated:
daily
navigation:
★ ★ ★ ★
content:
★ ★ ★ ★
readability:
★ ★ ★ ★
speed:
★ ★ ★ ★
US

online music space or representatives from major music labels via Real.

• Get a daily or weekly news email delivered to keep you up to date on Lars (Ulrich, of Metallica, for those not clued up on the Napster controversy) and company's latest suit.

OTHER STUFF

• Listen has a library of in-depth reports available through the research channel, but these are designed more for industry professionals, and you have to pay for access.

An authoritative, objective and intelligent resource for news and analysis of the burgeoning digital entertainment industry.

http://www.worldpop.com
Worldpop

Launched in May 2000, internet music pup worldpop has probably been the noisiest upstart in the online music space by netting a massive cross-media sponsorship of the official top 40 singles chart in May, and virtually taking over Ibiza this summer with a special microsite pushed on dazed pleasure-seekers through cyber-café's across the sun, sound and sex-drenched island.

The content on this bubblegum-bright site seems to have every mainstream music craze covered, with the latest pop-celeb news updated daily and weekly, often exclusive, interviews with the man, woman or avatar of the moment, compiled by seasoned music hacks.

COOL STUFF

• Next to news and Real-streamed interviews, a massive 16 channels offers UK album and single charts listings with Real samples, plus its own branded global top 40, a poptastic events calender, gossip columns, chatrooms, message boards, games and ticket and merchandise etail. You can't access CD retailing at worldpop – something to do with chart sponsorship rules – but otherwise, think Saturday morning TV without the naff presenters. Phew, pop pickers!

overall rating:	★ ★ ★ ★
classification:	mainstream pop and dance
updated:	several times daily
navigation:	★ ★ ★ ★ ★
content:	★ ★ ★ ★
readability:	★ ★ ★ ★
speed:	★ ★ ★ ★ ★
UK	

• A definitive guide to the major pop events, from festivals to star birthdays throughout the year. A place to plan your worship.

• Well-populated, fairly raucous debates go on in the worldpop chatrooms, although the message boards, especially the music physician Dr Pop's board, don't appear to have set the web alight, with zero responses to most posts. Also in the community section, pick up lots of naff pop prizes to swagger around with in the playground.

• The Ibiza microsite manages to portray the best of the summer hedonistic lifestyle on the island, complete with a sunset Webcam at the Pascha beach bar and a sweaty body one at the main Pacha club. Good all-round free pre-holiday Balearic news and events.

A comprehensive and innovative mainstream pop and dance site suitable for the 18-30 gossip-hungry and mad-for-it Brit crowd.

http://www.clubplanet.com
ClubPlanet

Quite a few sites have been put up over the last year or so claiming to be the one-stop shop for club news and listings online. This is the only site we came across that comes close to fulfilling the functionality the web is so perfect for, with its core function of searchable listings by city accompanied by useful news, club reviews and features.

A US launched site, Clubplanet has a UK section providing news and listings info for London only, but it is set to expand to further UK cities in the near future. Pick London from the dropdown menu of cities at the top of the adequately designed homepage, and you're taken into a tailored site for the capital, with news headlines hyperlinks as its main feature on the opening interface. Alternatively, you can access the six channel community and listings features on the right hand link menu. Some of the areas require you to register to gain access.

COOL STUFF

• Use the Club Search channel to seek out venues and facilities in London or in a range of US and European cities.

• Look for a job, a new love (via aplacetomeet.com) or a home on the classified pages of the Lounge channel. Also, there are fairly well-populated message boards and holidays to be won on the contest page. In other words, the usual community fare.

overall rating:	
★ ★ ★	
classification:	
UK hip-hop lifestyle	
updated:	
weekly	
navigation:	
★ ★ ★ ★ ★	
content:	
★ ★ ★ ★	
readability:	
★ ★ ★ ★	
speed:	
★ ★ ★ ★ ★	
UK	

• Listen to weekly updated DJ mixes via the ClubPlanet radio link on the homepage (you must have Windows Media Player downloaded for access).

COOL STUFF

• Access international clubland reviews and features, DJ profiles and virtual tours of New York and Miami clubs, and photos in the Word channel. You can also elect to buy a selection of releases by clicking through to ecommerce partner CDNow on the buy link at the end of each review.

Clubbers of the world unite! The best online guide to the London and US club scene.

http://www.spinemagazine.com

spinemagazine

Software: Flash

Nattily designed, the recently launched spinemagazine sets high standards with the first 'edition'. Claiming to be in it for the love, Spine proudly declares its underground roots, and promises that not only will it signal the end of paying hard cash for your music, but also let you know where the threads are at: 'The media is twisted and spine is here to set things straight. Spine is us. Spine is you. Welcome to the family...'

It appears to be doing nicely for now, with a clean and spacious interface that ranks with some of the best designed sites without resorting to heavy use of Flash animation. Read the latest news from the world of turntablist contests and where to get those rare Nike Air Max by following the news links, and check out some fairly hefty, nicely written hip-hop live and record reviews in the music section. Spine intends to expand its music coverage to drum'n'bass, house, garage and techno genres when it gets the foot soldiers. Ever fancied becoming a writer?

COOL STUFF

• A broad and useful range of interviews, reviews and top ten selections can be found in the music section.

overall rating:	★ ★ ★
classification:	UK hip-hop lifestyle
updated:	weekly
navigation:	★ ★ ★ ★ ★
content:	★ ★ ★ ★
readability:	★ ★ ★ ★
speed:	★ ★ ★ ★ ★
UK	

• A fantastic links page, taking you to more stylish corners of the web, although, possibly because it's a newbie, spinemagazine doesn't carry any audio links to accompany its reviews.

OTHER STUFF

• Fashion reviews and features, Graf action and interactive design pictures.

A subversive online magazine who claim their sole intent is to rip the spine out of the media. That, and tell you where to get the latest hot fashion Nike Airs.

OTHER SITES OF INTEREST

Clickmusic
http://www.clickmusic.co.uk
Launched in 1999 by former record label executives as the definitive portal for all music content online, Clickmusic goes some way towards meeting its objectives without quite having become the one-stop-window to the sonic surf it aims to be. However, owing to most music lovers' eclectic tastes, it would be fair to say that, of each portal mentioned in this section and beyond, Clickmusic does one of the best jobs. Its interface is bright, easy to navigate and attractive, it boasts some fun and useful features, and packs a useful, subject-prioritised search engine. Click probably includes some of the best UK links for music shopping, nationwide gig listings, and genre-specific sites housed within easy to read channels – such as shopping, listings and band guide channels. The playroom has innovative music business games, with a chance to win some top dollar prizes such as a scooter or portable digital music player.

E-dance
http://www.e-dance.co.uk
This is a useful independent news, review, listings and ecommerce resource site for the UK clubbing crowd. Completely independent, and still small enough to remember its roots, this site covers the world for the weekend hedonists from the ground up. Nice and solid, nice and easy.

music

NME
http://www.nme.com
This chapter would be incomplete without a mention of this site, owing to the paper version's legendary status in the UK pop, rock and indie scene, and the site's claim to be the 'UK's No.1 website'. One of the key factors in deciding which sites made the grade for inclusion here is their ability to offer a quality experience or function not readily available offline. Apart from the largely uninteresting, if expansive, message boards and chat room and the odd webcast, it is largely an online version of the weekly rag. It's clear that quite a hefty resource has been channelled into the site, and its daily-updated news, release and gig reviews, and interviews are informative if you don't want print on your hands from the paper version. Good for angst-ridden ex-indie kids, despite the lacklustre design.

AltaVista Entertainment
http://www.entertainment.altavista.com
Another wide-reaching window to the world of music online. Like most US grown portals, AltaVista hasn't quite got its music content up to scratch on its .co.uk site, but the dotcom site serves all the purposes for the novice and nit-picky explorer alike. Aside from the rather boring interface (broad web portals like this aren't in the business of being fresh and funky), AltaVista offers some useful category searches, and is regarded as delivering the widest reaching results of all search engines.

Get your ubiquitous AltaVista streaming and playing software, courtesy of stream specialist iCast, or a beta version of the Altavista Sonic Burner for creating CDs with all those lovely MP3s you've clogged up your hard drive with, via obvious links on the left column of the homepage.

New Media Music
http://www.newmediamusic.com
Basically a press release wire for news from new media music companies on new site launches and features, such as a new online radio channel added to a site. Subscribe to the daily or weekly email for a useful, at-a-glance update on new stuff. You could also take a look at Audiotoday.com for digital music industry news and views, and Musicdish.com and mi2n.com for wider industry news, US style.

HoboMusic
http://www.hobomusic.com
Aimed at the aspiring musician, this recently launched UK site aspires to be an online hub for the grass roots British music production business. Its features include daily updated pan-industry news and a comprehensive studio channel, which offers details of availability, facilities and online booking requests. The site also has industry jobs classifieds, the latest product reviews for musicians, studios, DJs and touring, and buying tips.

music

Platform Network

http://www.platform.net

This site was set up in 1996 by US design agency Tagworks as a launch pad into a range of beats, culture, style, and aggregated from a number of magazines, style leaders and retailers. Dubbing itself the Transglobal Urban Living portal, Platform takes from hip-hop, skate and snowboard culture to present a fully-networked, brightly presented resource for hearing and reading about latest releases and the buzz in US DJ culture, and hard to find threadz. Sites to look for include www.digitalbombing.com for rare beats and www.massappeal.com for breakbeat style and culture.

Music Mag

http://www.musicmag.com

This London based zine is not a bad online tool for the UK mainstream dance/clubbing scene. Packing in all the features you will come to expect, such as a message board and reviews, the site is only really worth the visit for its up-to-date news on dance events on and offline and releases, and its club search tool. Follow links in the clubbing channel and enter your town, preferred date and genre to get a substantial listing of a good cross-section of events, or follow the links to sister site www.crasher.co.uk for a searchable database of popular clubs and promoters nationwide. A useful nationwide virtual Time Out for major dance events.

The Wire
http://www.thewire.co.uk
The online version of the magazine that covers adventures in modern music, offers a cerebral look at the making of modern beats, jazz, breakbeats, modern classical and the music from the 'outer limits' and how it contributes to the fabric of the global community. The interface is unfussy and easy to navigate. It also has decent national and international listings of juicy fringe musical events such as the Carribean Summer Live and the Big Chill, details of the content and how to subscribe to the print version and get free CDs.

San Francisco Drum'n'Bass
http://www.sfdb.com
Linked with the US West Coast's thriving underground sites xlr8r.com and betalounge (see p.108), SFDB show they may have finally caught the UK grown beats bug. Read the latest news, check out biogs and photos of the movers and shakers and, most importantly of all, stream all the latest releases and mixes coming out of this fledgling scene.

Off Its Face
http://www.offitsface.com
Within the realm of dance music on the net, where some sites are getting huge amounts of investment for the provision of a virtually uninformative service, it is encouraging to come across a site such as this, where it is based purely on voluntary work.

The actual site is attractively arranged. Simplicity is the key; everything is visible and user-friendly. There are several links to other related sites with many different sources and information. Other than the music aspect of the site there are many sub-topics, including surfing, mountain biking, a miscellaneous page which has information on PC games, fonts, software and other downloadables. Finally, and most importantly, there are pages on that highly successful and internationally renowned club of footballing genius, Cardiff City. See, the site also has its comedic side. Great site, keep up the work.

The Skinny
http://www.skinny.com
The Skinny describes itself as the only resource for the 'exploding Do-It-Yourself generation'. We'll let you decide what that means, and if you're part of it. The site is slick, swift and packed with weekly features on the world's leading electronic music artists, record labels, clubs, and fashion designers. The content blends innovative text with visually stunning design and interface, in addition to syndicated live music feeds from around the net. Past features have covered Kruder & Dorfmeister, DJ Spooky, Orbital, Grooverider, 2xITF champ Vinroc, and many other intriguing musical personalities. Its genre news coverage will satisfy any scene aficionado, too.

e-commerce sites

Many sites throughout this book ostensibly have e-commerce elements. However, many of them either only really deal with US delivery, or don't have the best price and choice. The sites we have singled out for review in this chapter are sites which you should be able to get the best price, delivery and customer service as a UK resident for physical goods – CDs, tickets and merchandise. Therefore, unlike other chapter in this book, these sites have been chosen on their shopping functional values rather than stylish substance.

When planning this book, we aimed to include as many e-commerce sites as possible which offered alternative payment methods for creditcard-less under eighteens. However, although there is a lot of talk and experimentation going on in this area, especially within the music industry – who recognise many of their best customers aren't old enough to own a credit card – no solid and universal solution has been found.

music

overall rating:	★★★★★
classification:	gig & festival tickets
updated:	weekly
navigation:	★★★★★
content:	★★★★★
readability:	★★★★
speed:	★★★★★
UK	

http://www.aloud.com
Emap

Not being affiliated to any particular group of promoters or venue owning company, and focusing almost exclusively on music events, makes Aloud one of the most comprehensive and informative guides to gigs and special events (at medium to large venues) and large UK festivals. The event search by UK town even includes my small home town, Colchester. This site has been around for longer than most of its ticketing ecommerce rivals, a factor which, together with its ready made feed from sister media (radio station Kiss 100, magazines Q and Mixmag for example), means it does an impressive job.

The interface is bright, bold and easy to follow, using obvious symbols to indicate if an event still has tickets available, and the simple purchasing process can be done online via credit card or over the telephone. Added extras such as the reviews, the interactive forum for finding last minute tickets, and comments on a particular tour and links to further event information rank this site above the minimalist functionality found elsewhere.

COOL STUFF

• An easy-to-read festival calendar, with listings hyperlinked to ticket sales, line-up and location details. Also in the festivals channel – linked via the right hand menu on the homepage – you can sign-up for a festival update email, post your comments or find tickets to sold out events on the message boards and festival chatroom, and view the festival map showing exactly where each event is happening in Blighty!

• Emap brings together the strengths of their Mixmag 'Out There' team, Kiss 100, The Box and Bargainholidays.com to bring you listings, latest news, cheap package deals, and music videos from Ibiza and Ayia Napia on their beachbeats.com microsite, linked at Aloud.com via the right hand menu.

OTHER STUFF

• Catch up on the latest celebrity gossip and quotes, posted on the Entertainment news page by Aloud's sister magazine Heat.

• All the main festivals and gigs get live reviews on the corresponding pages, linked via the right hand menu. As with the festivals, you can pen your reviews on the message boards.

• Catch up on backdated festival and gig announcements on the news archive page.

• Be amazed at what the great British public are buying on the Aloud top sellers list. A gig in December by the late 1980s/early 1990s hippy-guitar-beat crossover success, The Wonderstuff, had sold out by mid-August!

An objective, thorough online window on mid- to large-sized gigs, venues and special events with simple booking.

music

overall rating:	★ ★ ★ ★ ★
classification:	ecommerce with a dance bias
updated:	daily
navigation:	★ ★ ★ ★
content:	★ ★ ★ ★
readability:	★ ★ ★ ★
speed:	★ ★ ★ ★ ★
US	

http://www.epitonic.com

Epitonic

Software: Realplayer, Liquid, Quicktime, Windows Media Player.

Epitonic really is a bright star amidst the murky legion of sites claiming to be the place to get your alternative sonic gratification. Unlike many of its competitors, the Epitonic crew really do seem to be in it for the love of the music and the cool new ways of experiencing it online. It's like they want to let you in on their little secret, rather than try to fleece you of your hard-earned cash as a main priority.

Don't let the US orientation put you off. Although it has yet to launch a .co.uk version (due online by the end of the year), it does have a few dudes searching out the cream of the UK leftfield scene for inclusion on the site. So don't be surprised if you find Carl Cox nestling nicely next to Gus Gus.

The coolest thing about this site is the range of ways you can 'try b4 you buy', from a 30 second sample to a full album stream on some titles. Furthermore, Amazon handles its ecommerce transactions and fulfillment. The web's best-known retailer may be a bit like Woolworths in style, but when it comes to a simple buying process and speed of delivery, they do deliver.

COOL STUFF

• Epicenter is the editor's pick of new material, and is rotated daily. This is the page for the uninitiated, and a good way of sussing out the Epitonic sound. Either read about and download information on individual albums or choose to stream sample tracks from all the Epitonic albums of the day.

• If you need a bit of I-candy to garnish your audio experience, click on the video channel at the top right of the homepage and browse the selection. The page has a built in Microsoft Winamp player, so no extra downloads are required to check them out. Plenty of advice about bandwidth and size of connections to steer you to the maximum little-screen viewing experience.

• Epitonic offers a choice of two radio channels – the Hip Hop Bandwidth Boom Bap with DJ Monkey or Epitonic Indie Rock, given up by the Wombat. Epitonic really have got this thing nailed down to three-click ease. Click on the Radio link on the right naviagation bar, choose your station, choose your MP3 player and you're groovin'. Fantastically, refreshingly simple.

• The software channel is a smashing section with a comprehensive guide to the best MP3 players on the web, complete with full reviews and download instructions. Just click on the Software link on the top right of the homepage. Nice and easy. Epitonic even has its own branded player, which you can easily download from the software of radio sections.

• One of the few legal and above board sites that lets you listen to an entire album for free – as a stream, of course. To own it, you still have to buy the conventional CD. But this section represents a major step forward on the part of the labels, who wouldn't have dreamt of letting more than a couple of beats go, streaming or no, a few months ago.

• Audio samples and information on new release and pre-release material. Essential if you've got to be one step ahead.

• The chance to win that limited edition album you thought you'd missed – check the win free stuff section for some innovative competitions.

• You know what you want, you know what you like, so get straight to the source via a simple artist/genre search engine. No nonsense.

Funky, thorough and simple to use, Epitonic is one of the best ecommerce resources for leftfield kids the web has to offer.

http://www.net4music.com

Net4Music

Software: Adobe Acrobat Reader

As with almost every other region of music ecommerce, there are many fledgling dotcoms offering download access to sheet music and MIDI files. Net4Music manages to make the grade as the only entry in this field in the Good Web Guide to Music. This is because, apart from offering a fringe service, it has been more successful than most in gaining rights to sell music from a good proportion of the world's major publishers. You are likely, therefore, to find the scores you're after here.

Digital distribution of scores and midi files is a superb interpretation of the web's commercial potential, and Net4Music is reassuringly professional and thorough in its attempts to explain how the site works. The New User page, linked at the top of the homepage, takes you through what you can expect from the site.

With over 60,000 sheet music and MIDI files on its books, and currently expanding at the rate of 10,000 a month of all styles plus informative and useful articles from musicians around the world, Net4Music is a fantastic resource for composers of all levels.

overall rating:	★★★★★
classification:	sheet music/midi-file downloads
updated:	weekly
navigation:	★★★★★
content:	★★★★★
readability:	★★★★
speed:	★★★★★
FR	

music

COOL STUFF

• Net4Music claims to offer the widest access to downloadable sheet music and MIDI files on the internet. Whether or not this is strictly true, with deals in place with such publishing giants as EMI, it certainly can't be far wrong.

• Read enlightening and informative articles in the Editorial section on such diverse and intellectual topics as the guide to the greatest musical cities in the world from the viewpoint of in situ musicians and advice on music academia.

• The On the Mike pages of the editorial channel have monthly archived advice and experiences from accomplished composers ranging from stage fright to advice relating to specific instruments.

• The backstage pages of the editorial channel has views and advice from music lawyers, manufacturers and artistic directors. You can also find informative commentary on a range of sheet music, delivery and expression methods and a chance to air your own views in the Editorial channel.

• The directory offers free listing and search access to its worldwide database of musicians, schools, retailers and affiliated professions.

OTHER STUFF

• Like most, the site offers a free email subscription to get the latest news, offers and feature details available at the site.

• The site can be viewed in five different languages and accepts 22 different currencies.

• The site will make any musicians material available, so send your compositions in if you think you're good enough!

A thorough and comprehensive sheet music and MIDI file download resource and reliable source of information for professional and amateur musicians.

music

overall rating:
★★★★
classification:
CD and DVD shopping
updated:
weekly
navigation:
★★★★
content:
★★★★
readability:
★★★★
speed:
★★★★
UK

http://www.amazon.co.uk
Amazon

Despite recent jitters in the market, Amazon isn't the most famous shopping site for nothing. The site's ease of use, clarity and comprehensive content, along with the subsequent speed of delivery and customer service, is first rate. They have the best track record in terms of credit security during the buying process, and although it's like the bland department store of ecommerce, rather than the quirky shop in a trendy part of London, it is surprising how deep and wide the store's catalogue extends beyond the expected mainstream chart releases.

Amazon has done more than most to iron out eshopping glitches, and all the details in terms of how many days it will take to reach you, the full price, label, catalogue number and rating are clearly listed before you have to take any further steps towards purchase. Amazon is more of a shopping paradise, if pure retail is your bag, than an untamed and scary web jungle.

COOL STUFF

• Amazon's stock is divided into 12 loose genres, which you can find via the browse categories channel. The categories include Lounge, Nostalgia & Exotica, Soundtracks, and Dance and Electronic.

• Each CD is reviewed by Amazon and can be reviewed by customers. Given the slightly lame absence of audio clips, it's useful to get some broad opinions from people who've shelled out already, although there's no way of knowing how many of the reviews are written by objective listeners!

• Visit the Recommendation Centre and read up on which albums several music journalists and industry luminaries have decided you really must own, separated into the usual genre category pages such as Rock or Dance & Electronic. You can also leave your email address in the box for weekly recommendations of new and re-released albums.

OTHER STUFF

• The new and upcoming releases channel glancingly reviews the biggest mainstream releases on the main page, or you can opt for a more in-depth listing of the new and forthcoming in the genre categories, clearly linked to the left of the page.

• If you have a specific artist or album in mind, or want to browse what they have in stock from your favourite label, the music search feature is simple to use.

With its experience and investment in shopping online, Amazon comes head and shoulders above other etailers, making it a must for tentative newbies and a surprisingly useful destination for finding obscure releases.

music

overall rating:	★ ★ ★ ★
classification:	CD, DVD and video shopping
updated:	weekly
navigation:	★ ★ ★ ★
content:	★ ★ ★ ★
readability:	★ ★ ★ ★
speed:	★ ★ ★ ★
GER	

http://www.uk.bol.com

BOL – Bertelsmann

Software: Real Player

Launched by German media giant Bertelsmann in 1998 as an online bookstore, and adding audio products in 1999, BOL (originally Books Online) is the only strong competitor to Amazon in terms of mainstream music retailing and quality of site and customer service. In fact there's little to choose between the two, apart from perhaps BOL's greater proximity to the local music scene and understanding of the challenges of European distribution.

With a bright, clean and attractive interface, BOL excels in easy navigation and transparent purchase process, as well as reliable and accountable credit handling and back-up customer support. There are no pre-release ordering facilities, but most mainstream new and back catalogue albums will be delivered within one to two working days. And, unlike Amazon, most albums have audio sample links attached to at least three tracks, hyperlinked with a music note next to the track listings.

COOL STUFF

• Unlike its main competitors, BOL carries charts for albums in the top 40, Indie, Dance, Rock, Jazz & Blues, and Classical charts, with links to buy.

Controversially, selected chart albums are available at the discount price of £9.99.

• All the album pages – BOL doesn't really do singles – are accompanied by comprehensive 'sleeve notes' detailing composers, collaborators and a brief history of the artist or group's career and previous releases, with the usual catalogue, price and track listing details.

• BOL stock is split into a massive 18 genre categories, including Easy Listening, Blues, New Age and even a Children's section. These can be browsed and searched in full via the link to the Browse genres channel at the top of the homepage.

• BOL gives each order an ID which can be used to check up on your order, which is especially useful if there is a hold up. Just click on the order status link at the top of the homepage.

• My-BOL – linked on the homepage – is a personalisation feature with which you can choose to have BOL present releases and special offers, tailored to your musical preferences, whenever you visit the site. If you sign up for this you will also receive regular emails with details of special offers and new releases according to your profile.

OTHER STUFF

• BOL differs from many ecommerce sites in that it offers editorial coverage such as features and interviews with artists. They are, however, likely to be about the ubiquitous artists of the moment, who already have features on many of the music portal sites, rather than exclusives.

• You can search its wares by artist, title and song writer in one or all formats (CD, cassette or box sets) and by whether it has audio clip samples.

• Find out which albums are moving fastest at BOL in the top sellers channel, linked at the top of the homepage.

• The artist of the week channel comprehensively reviews an up-and-coming buzz artist or group, picked up from the UK music and style press.

• If you want to beef up your CD collection with all-time classics, BOL offers its selections of must-have albums in the classics channel, linked at the top of the homepage.

BOL is a reliable European alternative to Amazon and is a good choice for speed of delivery, high standards of security and accountability for both new and back-catalogue CD and cassette albums.

http://www.boxman.co.uk

Boxman

Software: Real Player

Débuting with a small but successful Belgian site in 1996, music, video and games etailer Boxman has quickly expanded to have a country specific site in eight European countries. It purchased leading UK CD etailer Yalplay (IMVS) in late 1999, thus taking over a large slice of CD online purchasing in the UK. Boxman is significant and is included here because of its status as an ecommerce partner for many UK based music portals, including dotmusic.com and NME.com.

However, despite its unique pan-European online music retailing experience, it has not capitalised on its strengths. All the main music genres are easily accessed on the site, and the editors' picks are interesting, but the functionality is slightly flawed in that you can't easily search a particular genre. The content is sometimes strangely lacking; you can pre-order some major releases, but this section is not comprehensive. At the time of writing, one of the hottest album releases, from Mercury Prize nominee Badly Drawn Boy, is strangely absent. What's more, only new releases are reviewed and there is no facility for customer reviews or links to reviews on partner sites.

The site appears to have been built around the assumption that it will be visited more as an ecommerce partner to an editorial site, with all the corresponding info, rather than a destination

overall rating:	★ ★ ★ ★
classification:	CD, DVD and video shopping
updated:	weekly
navigation:	★ ★ ★ ★
content:	★ ★ ★ ★
readability:	★ ★ ★ ★
speed:	★ ★ ★ ★
BEL 🔒	

site in its own right. That said, if you can find what you want, you can expect a reliable buying and fulfillment process.

COOL STUFF

• If you are still into that early 20th century thing of feeling a weighty purchase, Boxman stocks a selection of albums that are available in vinyl. At the other end of the spectrum, the site has some titles available in Minidisc format. However, the vast majority of titles are CD format only.

• Boxman has a large fulfillment centre based on the continent, and they are fairly proficient on speedy delivery and secure purchase process.

• If you've already junked the computer, prefer your TV or have already moved on to wireless, you can shop Boxman via Sky Digital's Open shopping network or through BT's Wap Genie offering (in theory, anyway).

• You can buy a gift certificate and have the code sent directly to the lucky recipient via email.

An unimaginative, slightly less functional site than its main competitors, but can be relied upon for secure purchasing and speedy delivery for new and back catalogue albums.

http://www.hmv.co.uk

HMV

Software: Real Player

In keeping with the raison d'être that has made its high street business a success, HMV online employs the same irreverent, knowledgeable and insider feel to appeal to the more discerning music customer, as well as remaining accessible to the more general interest cats.

With a bright and bold interface, HMV's homepage is packed with offers, channels, reviews and features, which may appear a little too busy and intimidating to the uninitiated, reflecting their offline shopping experience. If you're wary of buying online, or find that shopping in a store does more for you than sitting in front of your computer like a zonehead, then HMV is a fantastic preparation resource, offering independent reviews of the best new releases across the board.

The storefinder feature can be useful for those sudden music-starved moments during trips to unknown cities. HMV is also about to debut some interesting multimedia features instore – such as custom CD instant burning booths for those ultimate compilations and broadband download booths to top-up your flash new music playing mobile or common old portable MP3 player.

overall rating:
★ ★ ★ ★
classification:
CD, DVD and video shopping
updated:
weekly
navigation:
★ ★ ★ ★
content:
★ ★ ★ ★
readability:
★ ★ ★ ★
speed:
★ ★ ★ ★
UK   R   🔒

music

COOL STUFF

• Good news for the online single-starved: HMV is one of the few sources to offer a full range of new singles.

• With HMV being knowledgeable about the UK scene, you'll find useful features, links and event information in each music genre channel, as well as useful reviews of all the latest releases, such as details on Ayia Napa and Notting Hill Carnival compilations in the soul'n'dance channel.

• Extensive opportunity to order albums and singles pre-release – follow the coming soon link at the top of the homepage.

OTHER STUFF

• To shop at HMV online you are required to register to get a customer ID, during which you can choose to receive emails with new release, special offer and event news.

• Each of the club-orientated genre channels has a chart compiled from hundreds of DJs' picks across the nation (Floor Fillers), most of which are pre-release and available for order.

• Check out what's hot with HMV shoppers on best top sellers page, which covers individual artist and compilation albums.

• The store recommends album, DVD and video releases on its HMV recommends page, linked from the top of the homepage. Don't expect any surprises, though, as it pretty much reflects the album charts.

HMV might be a bit light on the audio samples, but its a fantastic shopping resource for the general surfer (whatever that means) and the muso enthusiast alike.

music

overall rating:	★ ★ ★ ★
classification:	custom CDs
updated:	weekly
navigation:	★ ★ ★ ★
content:	★ ★ ★ ★
readability:	★ ★ ★ ★
speed:	★ ★ ★ ★
US 🔒	

http://www.musicmaker.com
Musicmaker

Software: Windows Media Player

Musicmaker is one of very few leaders in the field of custom CDs and secure digital downloads. Although it doesn't have anything like the spread of artists needed to make this a comprehensive site, it is cleanly presented and worth having a play with, as an example of things to come.

It is a well-known fact that the major labels have dragged their heels in embracing digital distribution, but this is set to change. Widescale commercial digital download trials with major artists have already got underway in the US, France and Germany, and should begin to appear in the UK very soon.

The majority of music on Musicmaker is by US artists, and it is one of the sites positioned to offer access to your favourites (legally) as they come online this side of the Atlantic. So have a little play, pick your tracks, listen to clips and let Musicmaker burn and mail your own chosen compilation, or create your own if you have the equipment, to prepare yourself for the world of music in the 21st century. The fact that the site is US-based means you may have to wait a little longer for delivery, but its UK competitor, www.razorcuts.com, has quite a limited available repertoire at this stage.

COOL STUFF

• Search one of 18 different genres for that eclectic compilation, or use the search at the top of the homepage to find if they have a particular artist or song title in the collection.

• The site carries a smattering of the latest music news and gossip.

A useful resource for creating custom CDs at home legally, and one to watch as major artists finally start distributing their music online for real.

music

overall rating:	★ ★ ★ ★
classification:	CD, DVD and video shopping
updated:	weekly
navigation:	★ ★ ★ ★
content:	★ ★ ★ ★
readability:	★ ★ ★ ★
speed:	★ ★ ★ ★
UK 🔒	

http://www.audiostreet.co.uk

Streets Online

Software: Real Player

Another ecommerce veteran, Audiostreet, part of Streets Online, has grown into a popular and trusted etailing venue since its launch in 1996. With a consistent track record in customer service and secure ecommerce, it is a progressively slick site which provides an enjoyable browsing and shopping experience. More imaginative than most, the interface is crisp and fairly simple to navigate, while the purchase process is easy compared to some other sites.

Often carrying selected albums at a steal, the site also offers enough added features, such as a buy and sell exchange page and live reviews, to persuade you to hang around longer than you usually might. Extensive charts, including a DJ floorfiller chart for dance genres are among the features that make this site stand out for the sophisticated sonic surfer.

COOL STUFF

• Audiostreet is the only credible online retailer in the UK to offer free MP3 downloads of selected tracks from artists doing the promotional rounds at the time. That might sound shockingly Napsteresque, but you should note that the downloads are configured to time-out after 30 days. Unless you're an accomplished hacker, you can't email them to your mates.

• If you access the site through the link at www.musicaid.org, 20 per cent of your cash will automatically go to UK-based charity World Music Foundation, who carry out projects to help needy children in third world countries. Visit the site to find out more.

• Audiostreet often ties up with some of the UK's distribution big boys to offer recently selected back catalogue albums for as little as £6.99.

• Unlike most ecommerce sites, Audiostreet has a latest music News and Gossip channel and a stunningly comprehensive features and live review archive for each genre.

• Find out what everyone else is buying in the Charts channel, with the full top 40, rock, dance, compilation, classical, jazz & blues, classical and indie top tens.

• Audiostreet's new release recommendations in the genre channels are refreshingly off-the-beaten track and usually a good bet. That said, running club and gig listings in the genre channels would be a good idea if they were up-to-date.

• Music video samples are available in the Digital channel, which is linked at the top of the homepage. It's also worth keeping an eye on this channel for new access functionality, such as video on demand and full range downloads.

• Streetsonline is WAP enabled.

music

OTHER STUFF

• Check out the new-releases channel, linked at the top of the homepage, for a full uncomplicated list of the current and following week's album releases, plus links to pre-order.

• Search by artist, album title or label for specifics.

• Sign up for an occasional email update on the latest general releases tailored to the genre of your choice.

• Link to a selection of mainstream online radio stations via Streets online broadcast channel, linked at the top of the homepage. Stations include Classic FM and Planet Rock.

A slick, pleasant surf through the world of music ecommerce with few stones left unturned.

http://www.ticketline.co.uk

Ticketline

Ticketline started life 30 years ago as the one-stop source for tickets to concerts and football matches in the North West of England. It has since matured into selling tickets for all size of music, theatre and football events in the region and major happenings nationally. Debuting with online booking in March 2000, Ticketline has been a relative latecomer to the web, but seems to have used its late start wisely with a slick, surprisingly attractive and more detailed site than its major competitors.

Events can be browsed by category (festival, jazz concert), date, venue, or location, and are clearly marked with symbols indicating if tickets are available, or if an event has been cancelled. Although this site will only be useful for the major capacity venue and major acts' gigs – it only handles major artist gigs out side of the north west – it stands out for the extra thought put into presentation and added value content, such as links to artist and event reviews and, a discussion and review forum where you can pick up and submit reviews and requests for tickets for a sold out gig.

COOL STUFF

• A message board forum area, linked via the top menu on the homepage, where you can moan, praise and sell or buy tickets to a sold out gig. Hallelujah for a bit of thought on extra resources and information, tuned into what the web can deliver!

overall rating:
★ ★ ★ ★
classification:
gig & festival tickets
updated:
weekly
navigation:
★ ★ ★ ★
content:
★ ★ ★ ★ ★
readability:
★ ★ ★ ★ ★
speed:
★ ★ ★ ★
UK 🔒

OTHER STUFF

• The news pages update on extra ticket availability and new concert announcements, which you can also elect to receive notification of via a free email subscription.

An attractive, reliable and easy-to-use ticket purchasing and event information resource with some useful added extras.

http://www.ticketmaster.co.uk

Ticketmaster

This entertainment ticketing veteran finally moved onto the web last year. With 18 years of experience of offline ticketing, the company has established enough relationships with artist management and venues to provide a comprehensive coverage of major gigs, festivals and club nights.

The interface is bright, breezy and easy to read, if not particularly slick. The obvious search and four-step purchase process should be easy enough for the most uninitiated surfer but as usual, under 18s will have to borrow the parents' plastic. Gigs, split into rock and pop, jazz, or country, are listed by artist name, while club and festival events can be found by browsing the clubs and dance channel via club/event name.

overall rating:	★★★★
classification:	gig & festival tickets
updated:	weekly
navigation:	★★★★
content:	★★★
readability:	★★★
speed:	★★★★
UK 🔒	

COOL STUFF

• A free email subscription will keep you updated weekly or monthly on new events listed. Unfortunately, however, this feature can't be tailored to suit your particular tastes.

OTHER STUFF

• Latest news pages details recently announced events across the Ticketmaster remit, including comedy and musicals as well as gigs and festivals.

• If you need to know what's hot with Ticketmaster types, click on the top 25 events via the link on the right of the homepage.

• The featured events page – linked on the right of the homepage – gives full details and links, such as a full festival line-up. Having said that, only a select list of events gets this treatment, making Ticketmaster, as with TicketWeb, more of an end-use buying tool than a research resource.

A comprehensive and reliable national mainstream, ticket ecommerce resource.

http://www.ticketweb.co.uk

TicketWeb – CitySearch/McKenzie Group

overall rating:
★ ★ ★ ★

classification:
gig & festival tickets

updated:
weekly

navigation:
★ ★ ★ ★

content:
★ ★ ★

readability:
★ ★ ★

speed:
★ ★ ★ ★

UK 🔒

Ticketweb.co.uk was launched last year by a US dotcom giant in partnership with the owner of the Shepherds Bush Empire and the Brixton Academy, the McKenzie Group. TicketWeb is a sharp, fiercely functional ticket transaction site with no frills, specialising in simplicity and no fuss processes. The interface is unimaginative, but effective for the job in hand. This site is not a resource, however, for browsing event information. There are no details listed other than the title of the event, date, venue and ticket price, and, strangely, no links to sites with further information about a particular gig.

But if you already know you want to go to an event, and it's just a case of booking, then TicketWeb is a thorough and reliable resource for online booking. Search over 50 mid to large venues for major artist gigs – from the Forum in Kentish Town, London to the Leadmill, Sheffield, to the Glasgow Barrowlands Ballroom – or click on one of the listed venues to find out who is booked over the coming months.

COOL STUFF

• Use the search on the homepage to find the event you're interested in, either by date, artist or venue, select the number and type of tickets and whether you want the tickets sent to you or want to pick them up at the venue, and bash the plastic. Easy as ABC.

• You can click on any of the venues to discover upcoming gigs – most of the nation's popular venues are included.

Not a browsing tool, with no extra information on events, or links, but it does do its job efficiently.

OTHER SITES OF INTEREST

CDNOW

http://www.cdnow.com

Once the darling of successful ecommerce, alongside Amazon, CDNOW was recently bought by BOL parent Bertelsmann after it hit financial difficulties. Although it always had ambitions to expand its operations fully to the UK and Europe, apart from opening a European shipping centre, CDNOW never really managed to crack the UK market in terms of a tailored, localised content offering and overcoming fulfilment difficulties. Now that it has a European parent, it may yet upscale its service in Europe. For the time being, we recommend you choose one of the other general music shopping sites reviewed in this section over CDNOW so as to lower the risk of paying import charges after waiting longer than necessary! Apart from actual shopping, CDNOW can be useful for its extensive interviews and reviews, and perhaps to discover new music through its 22 channel CDNOW radio feature.

Blackstar

http://www.blackstar.co.uk

Probably the first serious and competent UK video etailer, Blackstar has consistently picked up praise and even awards for both its breadth and depth of video and DVD stock and customer service performance. For the majority of new and available back music video releases, click on video browse

music ──────────────────────────────

followed by the music and performing arts channel on the left-hand side of the homepage, and choose one of six general categories, all of which are subdivided into extensive sub-categories such as Christmas (!), reggae and jazz within the popular music section. Hitherto dominated by film, music DVD releases are on the increase, with quite a few titles expected to hit the stores over Christmas. If you've got a player, Blackstar offers a 30 per cent discount on many releases if you pre-order, which is nice. Expect to see video on demand features as broadband rolls out in the UK over the next few months.

The Dance Music Resource Pages
http://www.juno.co.uk
Dubbing itself the Dance Music Resource Pages, this no-frills British site is a comprehensive guide and shopping destination for all new domestic and import dance vinyl releases at reasonable prices.

whatsonwhen
http://www.whatsonwhen.com
This site is an excellent resource if you're planning a holiday or city break and want to find out what's going down before you travel, or, indeed, if you want to plan a holiday destination or dates around a festival or gig. Well-designed and easy to use, whatsonwhen is worth a look before any trip abroad, or even for searching out unusual or fringe events in the UK.

Catapult

http://www.catapult.co.uk

A nice little vinyl shopping site set up by Cardiff independent dance store Catapult in 1998. Its wide range of trance, techno and drum'n'bass should make it a mecca for bedroom DJs (you know who you are). Also, check out www.futurebeatmusic for exhaustive dance vinyl and CD stock and reliable online ordering.

Netsounds

http://www.netsounds.com

Netsounds was formed in 1998 to bring together and combine the catalogues of many different dealers, shops, mail order companies and collectors. It forms a single giant catalogue, enabling customers to search in one place for that hard-to-find or deleted music item. Netsounds is not a retailer but a marketplace and facilitator. The site design is brash rather than svelte, but it is useful as a one-stop shop for buying a wide selection of music online from thousands of competing outlets in the UK. It is also accountable in terms of allowing customers to post notification if they experienced bad service from a particular source, which is attached to information on that store's page, and it doesn't allow back ordering. Over 200 partners participate, from private collectors in Australia, to rare period classics purveyors in the Netherlands ,to up-to-date rare grooves specialists in Sheffield.

downloading music

This chapter deals with where it's really at online. The reason the Internet lives, thrives and prospers is because it connects people from all corners of the globe with access to a computer and a modem. It allows them to share data – whether a text document, MP3, or picture Jpeg file – and ideas instantly, and empowers everyone to air their opinions, ideas, and creativity. This is revolutionary. In the same way email has transformed many workplaces, the ability to encode and compress a piece of audio or visual media into a file that can be accessed, streamed, downloaded and sent electronically to your mates is transforming people's access and experience of music. When you have your MP3 player in your hand, which you've just loaded up with all your favourite music whether encoded from your existing music collection, or, more likely, from a download site, you will understand. When you can link your stereo or your mobile phone to your broadband connected computer or television and instantly access new music you will really start to dig the real power of the Internet. Instant music how you want it, when you want it and where you want it.

This isn't just a new format like Minidisc; it actually changes the whole structure of how music is delivered, accessed and experienced, and subsequently the entire nature of how the music industry will work in the future. Many established traditional companies with control of offline distribution networks have been slow to adapt to the challenges of online distribution and have paid the price through ultimately damaging lawsuits against people who have gone ahead and built sites to meet customer demand for complete access to all music online – such as MP3.com, and more famously Napster. As you read this, at least two of the big five record companies (EMI and Sony) will be making some music available for download via a variety of retail sites in this country. However, at the time of writing, there was still no 'legal' viable alternative to Napster et. Al. in this country.

This is the Good Web Guide to Music, and our aim is to scour the web for the best sites that meet a set of common objectives, so you don't have to. As a result, Napster is included as one of the few sites that allow access, and will probably continue to do so in some form or another pending the ongoing lawsuit in the US. The majority of sites reviewed are ones that give you access to top-quality streaming audio, because, quite simply, they are not hampered by the same restrictions. So, plug in, sit back and enjoy the revolution.

music

overall rating:	
★ ★ ★ ★ ★	
classification:	
streaming audio destination site	
updated:	
weekly	
navigation:	
★ ★ ★ ★ ★	
content:	
★ ★ ★ ★	
readability:	
★ ★ ★ ★	
speed:	
★ ★ ★ ★ ★	
US	

http://www.betalounge.com

The Beat Lounge – Network Syndicate

Software: Windows Media Player.

The Beta Lounge is a fairly new dance music showcase transmitted live over the internet every Thursday, 8pm to 12am Pacific time, from the San Francisco studios of the Network Syndicate. All the shows are archived immediately after the live event and are available on this site throughout the week. Live events range from DJ mixes at industry happenings, such as Germany's Popkomm, to broadcasts from SF club Eklecktic.

With a stylish, bold and simple interface, each section of the site, be it live shows, past shows, MP3s, shop (expect to pay up to £10 for overseas delivery of clothes or music) or links, is easily reached via the constant menu across the top of each page. Crucially, the route to listening is a simple three-click process, and the audio streams are consistent in their quality.

COOL STUFF

• The links channel contains one of the most comprehensive lists of stylish, beats-driven ezine, video and audio and download sites. Happy surfing.

OTHER STUFF

• The Beta Lounge compiles a weekly top five.

• A chat area, of course, but no bulletin/message boards.

• You can stream a variety of individual tracks in the MP3 channel, although they aren't available for full download storage.

An oasis of style, simplicity and sonic sophistication in a galaxy of pretenders, for those with eclectic tastes in electronica.

music

overall rating:	★ ★ ★ ★
classification:	event webcasting
updated:	weekly
navigation:	★ ★ ★ ★ ★
content	★ ★ ★ ★
readability:	★ ★ ★ ★
speed:	★ ★ ★ ★ ★
UK R	

http://www.doneanddusted.com
Done and Dusted

Software: Windows Media Player and Flash

Done and Dusted is a good-looking site from the creative wells of the music TV production company of the same name. This is a fledgling effort and although it is achingly slick in its design and Flash-based navigation, like Playlouder, it is still in the process of perfecting the webcast experience. Perhaps because of its offline contacts, Done and Dusted secured rights to many of the Summer 2000 events, all of which are presented here within their own multi-channel, individually styled microsites.

Registration is required to view the free content, which ranges from clips of most acts performing on the main stages, to scenes from the burger van. Admittedly, the site hasn't quite got it done and dusted yet; a few of the major acts still aren't available for viewing, and in some instances only a small segment of their performance was available for viewing. Furthermore, some of the scheduled artists failed to make an appearance, and users on the T in the Park message board derided the coverage of the festival as being by media tarts for media tarts.

The site is young, though, and we feel it has obvious and meaningful potential, and should be given the benefit of the doubt while it gets over its teething problems. Current coverage includes T in the Park, V2000, MTV Ibiza, and Creamfields.

COOL STUFF

• Each event features webcasts of the majority of artists performing on the main stages, an amusing collage of crazy crowd kids, and dispatches from unlikely corners of the site such as the chip van, the portaloos and wherever else they feel like capturing for web history.

• You don't have to download the Windows Media Player to run the webcasts; they will be automatically launched within your browser.

OTHER STUFF

• News from the festival artist massive via Channelfly.com, in the festival latest channel.

• A full schedule for each event covered is listed on the line-up pages within each event microsite.

• A pretty active message board, populated mainly by dissatisfied punters, especially for T in the Park. It seems that Done and Dusted have a little way to go yet.

An embryonic site which shows great potential, and already has exclusive access to some major events.

music

overall rating:	★ ★ ★ ★ ★
classification:	live streaming
updated:	weekly
navigation:	★ ★ ★ ★ ★
content:	★ ★ ★ ★
readability:	★ ★ ★ ★
speed:	★ ★ ★ ★ ★
US	

http://www.dublab.com
Dublab

Software: Real player, Flash.

Dublab is an LA-based collective of DJs and artists who see themselves as dedicated to the growth of new, positive music and culture, creating a vibe rather than a format. Dublab refuse to be labelled within one genre, preferring to play whatever they feel defines a moment or movement through the net underground. Whether you buy their ambitious aim to create a global community of sound-based culture or not, Dublab is worth an exploratory listening visit for its sophisticated aesthetic and serious dedication to sonic and visual pleasure.

Dublab's DJs are seasoned professionals who work more or less full-time, creating sounds and webcasts for the site. Their favourite records include material from artists as diverse as Aphex Twin, Jazzanova, Bob Marley, The Pixies, Ray Keith, Roy Ayers and Bon Jovi. This is a site without playlists and commercial sympathy, unlike traditional radio and its online manifestations.

COOL STUFF

• Records the excellent Clubstereophonic.com outputs.

• Extensive links to some of the most beautiful, innovative, unconventional and weird corners of cyberspace.

OTHER STUFF

• Text, audio and visual features on random artists, labels and underground 'scenes' from cities around the world in the Baby Mammoth section of the Incubator channel, linked via the spraycan graphic on the home page.

• Artist, visual and text profiles in the gallery section of the incubator channel. Updated monthly.

• In addition to the live and archived cybercasts, there is a chat area, which seems to have a strangely low population considering the like-minded music people mantra.

• Dublab top 30 chart in the Labrats channel. Also to be found in this channel is a full profile of the Dublab hypothesis, crew, DJs and visual gallery of collaborators. Always nice to know who you're dealing with.

A site which produces an eclectic and original range of sounds, with many gems amongst them.

music

overall rating:
★ ★ ★ ★ ★

classification:
streaming destination site

updated:
weekly

navigation:
★ ★ ★ ★ ★

content:
★ ★ ★ ★

readability:
★ ★ ★ ★

speed:
★ ★ ★ ★ ★

US

http://www.groovetech.com
Groovetech

Software: Real Player

Unlike most of the sites reviewed in this chapter, Groovetech doesn't have masses of pages bursting with eclectic content. It focuses primarily on the Seattle and San Francisco underground, house and beats scenes, and earns its place here for having some of the most diverse and consistently excellent quality live broadcasts on the web. This site represents a true centre for commitment to webcasting as a serious sonic medium.

Rather than attempting to spread itself thinly over many musical bases, Groovetech focuses on creating a community around non-commercial dance genres, creating access to excellent live broadcasts and archives as well as a secure and reliable route to obtaining many rare imports. The interface is clean, stylish and easily navigated, and the streams are simply activated. True style, real sounds – it's safe to turn up the volume.

COOL STUFF

• The Groovetech listening lab has listings of all the latest releases throughout its genres. Particularly useful for getting hold of rare imports, sourced via its London office.

• Active chat area in the Community channel, and an informative bulletin board with postings from both sides of the Atlantic.

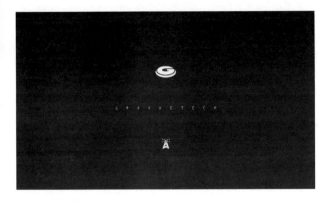

OTHER STUFF

• Some useful if not extensive links to online audio resources and some label sites.

A must-listen streaming and ecommerce resource for followers of the mellow dance underground community.

music

overall rating:	★ ★ ★ ★ ★
classification:	streaming & information network
updated:	weekly
navigation:	★ ★ ★ ★ ★
content:	★ ★ ★ ★
readability:	★ ★ ★ ★
speed:	★ ★ ★ ★ ★
CAN	

http://www.theiceberg.com
The Iceberg

Software: Realplayer, Flash

The Iceberg is the opening window to an extraordinarily rich, funky and stylish slice of sonic web action. Although it is based in Toronto, Canada, the Iceberg network is one of the few sites that understands and attempts to serve its global reach. The three streaming channels invite you to click your time zone on the world map to ensure all schedule information is configured to where you're at, which is a simple, effective feature.

The network consists of three alternative live and archive streaming channels – 1Groove, 2Kool4radio and Illnoiz – that cover three genres and are independently designed, both aesthetically and content-wise, to fit the music style. As you roll the mouse over the different site logos on the Iceberg page, a brief flava and ingredients are displayed, while clicking on one will open the particular site in a separate window. The only drawbacks are that shows are only archived for a week and you can't download any of them – Iceberg respect their creators!

The two other Iceberg sites offer extra services, with Primetickets linking to the fantastic global Pollstar database of concerts and the Deeper ezine offering a free email subscription to news, gossip and updates from across the network. Whether you're into pop, indie and, especially, hip-hop, soul, rare groove, roots and reggae, the painstakingly detailed, nattily designed and effortlessly cool Iceberg network should have a sonic truffle for your delectation. A rare box of treats.

1Groove.com

Dubbing itself One World Under 1Groove, 1Groove.com offers news, information and live shows featuring interviews and mixes with DJs from around the globe, specialising in every thing from ambient to trance, house to techno and hardcore to drum'n'bass. Think DJ Food and Ninja Tune's Kev & PC.

COOL STUFF

• Probably one of the best-designed music sites online, 1Groove sports a minimalist, stylish and fun interface for pure surfing pleasure. Once into the water bottle, click on the spinning atoms to get through to Europe and then London (or Ibiza!) to get club and event listings and domestic time broadcast schedules.

• Full instructions on the where, what and how of hooking up your PC to your dusty old stereo for supersonicsurfsound - located in the Direct Access section of the Club Culture channel. Also available in the Hook Up channel of 2kool4radio.

• Check out house or trance-related news in the psst! section of the Club Culture channel.

• See the faces behind the sounds in the Direct Access channel.

2kool4radio.com

Ambitiously describing itself as the Promised Land of Music, 2kool offers alternative, indie, punk, hip hop, loungecore and more sonic treasures from the leftish fringe.

COOL STUFF

• Listen to archived interviews with the likes of Travis, Kid Koala, Stereophonics, Red Hot Chilli Peppers, Moby and DJ Food in the Interviews channel of 2kool4radio. One of the most eclectic selections of international artists on the net.

• Listen to live broadcasts from the likes of Super Furry Animals or watch events such as Vince Carter's birthday bash in the live events channel.

• If it sounds like your idea of fun, in the game channel you can put in your birthday details to get a to-the- second countdown of how long you have before official retirement age!

illnoiz.com

Attempting to provide online 'urban' entertainment for a global audience, the Ill Noiz Network line-up includes Hip Hop, R&B, Reggae, Soca, Latin, Dancehall and Soul from both the under and overgrounds. Live hosted shows featuring music mixes, video and audio interviews roll 24 hours a day, 7 days a week. Originally a six-hour segment on 2kool4radio.com, Ill Noiz has expanded to continuous broadcasts of challenging and eclectic shows, exploring all aspects of black music and culture. Net radio with real attitude.

The programs include: Calypsoca Summit, a fusion of music and culture around the Soca genre, featuring artist profiles, island exposures and the roots of the music; El Niño, a wide variety of Latin music and information; Play My S#!t, designed to give independent and unsigned artists exposure, and covering R&B, Hip-Hop, Rap, Reggae, Soca, Calypso, Gospel, and Dub Poetry; Rub-A-Dub, reggae time with Deadly Hedley; Tie it Up, which offers culture and entertainment from a female perspective; and several others.

COOL STUFF

• Check out the cute introductory movie, which outlines sounds, collaborators and labels on the Ill Noiz site.

• Design your own tag and enter the contest to win cool bits in the Ill Noiz features channel.

OTHER STUFF

• Get an overview of all the programme slots in your timezone in the weekly schedules window.

• Check out the weekly Ill Noiz top ten across its station network in the top ten window.

• The Help channel gives a pretty comprehensive FAQ on trouble shooting with the Real player and the streams.

• Email links to tech support and service comments via the links in the top menu on the homepage.

PrimeTicket.net

This channel links you directly to Pollstar.com – an online global database run by the long-established Anglo-American specialist – industry publisher Pollstar. Search for mid to large-sized concerts, gigs and club nights by city, venue or artist. You can't book tickets here, but there is an exhaustive list of gigs.

COOL STUFF

• With 36,950 events and over 5,000 artists playing worldwide, Primeticket certainly covers all its bases.

• Intelligent industry, internet, and tour news.

Deeper

Deeper magazine is a free monthly email newsletter covering all Iceberg specialities – from pop to latin to reggae – with the claim that it's for cats who like to know what's hip so that they can impress their friends.

A site with exceptional design and global vision, with channels which cater for all musical tastes.

music

overall rating:	
★ ★ ★ ★ ★	
classification:	
free MP3 sharing resource	
updated:	
daily	
navigation:	
★ ★ ★ ★ ★	
content:	
★ ★ ★ ★	
readability:	
★ ★ ★ ★	
speed:	
★ ★ ★ ★ ★	
US	

http://www.napster.com
Napster

Software: Any MP3 player.

A Californian computer studies student, dubbed Nappy-head by his mates, dreamed up this site – hence the name. In case you've been living under a stone, Napster is a piece of free software that, once downloaded, allows any user to browse the MP3 collections stored on fellow users' hard drives. Simply type in an artist name or song/album title in the search engine on the search music page and you will be presented with a list of available MP3 files belonging to other users matching your request, sorted by each owner's speed of connection. You select one or more from the list and then select download.

The downside? Well, one MP3 file can take from three to 15 minutes to download, according to the speed of your connection and the person you 'share' with. And if you don't happen to have oodles of spare cash to splash out on portable MP3 players or the latest wired-for-music mobile phone, or don't think it's that cool to listen to your music collection through your tinny plastic PC speakers, owning an MP3 archive would be largely useless.

US college students have tackled this particular problem by buying recordable CDs (CD-R) and hardware which 'burns' the files onto them, but that can be expensive and time-consuming. What's more, the Napster network relies on human competence, meaning that you can end up with half a song when the user you're downloading from decides to log out before you're done.

Even so, Napster remains totally revolutionary. Designed for the wired teen 'digerati', it has let the kids show the music business that they expect unrestricted access to their favourite bands and their music via the internet, and sent many music industry cats into a spin. Napster is currently embroiled in a lawsuit with the Recording Industry Association of America, and whilst the consensus is that Napster won't be shut down, it may not remain free for much longer.

COOL STUFF

• Join in some of the most amusing rants, debates and lighthearted chats on the web via the Community channel.

• The New Artist program was added recently as a bit of an afterthought, but is probably one of the most effective places to post unsigned material.

A cool site for a revolutionary piece of software. So revolutionary, in fact that that the corporate music bigwigs would like to see it disappear.

music

overall rating:	★ ★ ★ ★ ★
classification:	webcast & information
updated:	weekly
navigation:	★ ★ ★ ★ ★
content:	★ ★ ★ ★
readability:	★ ★ ★ ★
speed:	★ ★ ★ ★ ★
UK	

http://www.playlouder.com

Playlouder

Software: Real Player.

One of the few Brit sites attempting to hold up the sonic interactive media stakes this side of the Atlantic, the fledgling Playlouder sparkles with promise. Having become one of the few sites to obtain official webcasting rights to Glastonbury 2000 a mere two months after launching, Playlouder has demonstrated that it has the links and the nous needed to try and make something of live music entertainment online.

Webcasting festival and live events in the narrowband era is, quite frankly, not compelling, especially when, with an event like Glastonbury, you can watch it far more comfortably on your reliable, non-jerky TV screen. But we're talking potential here. Playlouder, with its determination and commitment to the medium, is one to watch.

COOL STUFF

• Although the technology isn't really there yet, once you have your permanent broadband connection installed, Playlouder should become a reliable destination for large event webcasts.

• Playlouder radio consists of featured artists' tracks, which are worth a listen.

OTHER STUFF

• A light-hearted, fairly amusing take on the UK music news and gossip of the day.

• Regular giveaway offers for gig tickets and band merchandise.

• Occasional video/audio exclusives, usually from Beggars Banquet artists.

• Weekly updated interview features on the artists cutting up the leftish commercial scene. Think along the lines of St Etienne, Badly Drawn Boy and Coldplay.

An amusing and interactive sonic and visual dispatch from the best of the slightly left-of-centre UK music scenes.

music

overall rating:
★ ★ ★ ★ ★

classification:
streaming audio & video

updated:
weekly

navigation:
★ ★ ★ ★ ★

content:
★ ★ ★ ★

readability:
★ ★ ★ ★

speed:
★ ★ ★ ★ ★

US

http://www.sputnik7.com
sputnik7

Software: Realplayer/Windows Media Player, Flash.

Chaired by the legendary Island records founder Chris Blackwell, this site had to be the bomb. Happily for the sonic connoisseurs, it doesn't disappoint. Although the site features some emerging artists from Blackwell's Palm Pictures label, the award-winning sputnik7 doesn't sink to discrimination; some of the world's finest new and established artists are represented in glorious audio-visual technicolour, set against a stylish Flash-heavy web interface.

It's not just restricted to music either; sputnik7 is a broadcast network offering a sophisticated mix of independent music, film, and anime programming via interactive Video Stations, Audio Stations, Videos on Demand, and Digital Downloads. Chat, music ecommerce, requests, video ratings, artist and information functionality are all built into the broadcast windows, providing a high level of rare, uninterrupted and interactive entertainment. Seeing is believing: this site sets new standards for online music content.

COOL STUFF

• The quality and breadth of content on this site is pure class, whether you want to listen to remixed Marley tracks, or watch the latest Lucy Pearl video.

• The featured content section of the music channel is updated weekly with four new features and free video-on-demand links to related content.

• The video stations within the Music channel currently offer three genre channels, covering Ska, pop/rock, electronic, hip-hop without borders, and reggae artists and culture. Nice.

• You will find a surprisingly large selection of free MP3 and video downloads in the corresponding section of the Music channel – from Underworld to Divine Styler – but most are emerging artists.

OTHER STUFF

• The radio channels are provided by partner Musicchoice.com. Choose between seven cover-all-bases channels, automatically streamed via your browser in a separate window. This section of the site can be uncharacteristically slow, however.

Real-time interactive audio and video streams and downloads from some of the world's finest new and established artists. A rare treat.

music

overall rating:	★ ★ ★ ★ ★
classification:	streaming video
updated:	irregular
navigation:	★ ★ ★ ★ ★
content:	★ ★ ★ ★
readability:	★ ★ ★ ★
speed:	★ ★ ★ ★ ★
US	

http://www.vmations.com
Sudden industries

Software: Flash and Shockwave.

A good business plan in the eyes of a venture capitalist does not necessarily make for a music lover's dream destination. A company may crow about having trillions of radio channels on their site, but if 99 per cent of those are posted by your granny's best friend or the weird bloke at number 29, it's hardly going to be compelling listening.

Describing itself as the net ready video alternative, Sudden Industries has the sum total of 10 artists' videos available on their site currently. Numbers aren't the point; these should grow. The fact is that these videos, which have been especially created for the medium, are presented with such style and attention to detail that the site is setting a much needed example.

Unusually, and refreshingly, each animation or film, or artist/label information – selected via the various dropdown menus around the video frame – appears within the main frame on this minimal site. This means that you need not get hopelessly lost jumping around from page to page. Keeping everything within easily navigated frames on one page is such a simple concept, but perhaps because it takes a bit more work, it is rarely found. At the time of writing, artists represented in the vmation style include industrial innovators Kraftwerk, Nine Inch

Nails and The Mighty, Mighty Bosstones. Vmations want to kill the video star.

COOL STUFF

• Search for a vmation by artist, label or track title.

• An extensive help section for technical difficulties with the site.

This site is rare in managing to avoid the quantity-over-quality trap. That's not to say that it won't grow in size, but if what's there gives a clue to future development, the content will be carefully selected.

music

overall rating:
★ ★ ★ ★ ★

classification:
live audio/visual webcasting

updated:
daily

navigation:
★ ★ ★ ★ ★

content:
★ ★ ★ ★

readability:
★ ★ ★ ★

speed:
★ ★ ★ ★ ★

US

http://www.wiredplanet.com
WiredPlanet

Software: Real Player, Flash.

For a first-rate introduction to the art of streaming media, try WiredPlanet. Aside from its 14 in-house stations – from non-commercial indie channel Flipside to downtempo beats and grooves station The Future Lounge – you can link to a wide and eclectic pick of shows from around the web, hosted by such sites as DJMixweb and Epitonic.com.

The site offers three ways to connect to its stations, via a friendly and fun interface. Simply click on the Listen button and choose to listen via your browser, your preferred Player, or the WiredPlanet customised player. The site implores you to download its own player for both full sonic pleasure and for the purposes of experimentation, but it really isn't necessary. The quality of sound is just as good via browser connection.

Where WiredPlanet is really innovative is in its customisation features. You can either elect to have the site remember your preferences and create tailored programming, or click on the link to add a track to your own personalised playlist as you go along.

COOL STUFF

• A total of 28 stations to choose from, covering every genre imaginable. As you get used to WiredPlanet and want to create your own programming, follow the simple player download instructions and become master of your digital sonic destiny.

• Each track played is accompanied by an extensive biog and sleeve art information, which pop up in a separate window when clicked on, in the player window.

• If you need to own a track or hear an album, the buy button in the player window will link you through to Amazon.

• If you think you've created a supa-fine mix, you can add it to the Listener Stations channel and send links to your mates. You don't need to know how to work a record player to gain playground DJ kudos. Just click on the interact button at the top of the homepage to get the beginners Mystation builder kit.

• The WiredPlanet player features a rating slider, allowing you to rate a track for future spins: 10 for love it, 0 for don't ever play it again. Nice touch.

OTHER STUFF

• Chat to other listeners via the chat button on the player.

A great site for beginners and enthusiasts of any genre of music.

music

overall rating:	★ ★ ★ ★
classification:	live webcasting and archives
updated:	daily
navigation:	★ ★ ★ ★
content:	★ ★ ★ ★
readability:	★ ★ ★ ★
speed:	★ ★ ★ ★
US	

http://www.digitalclubnetwork.com
Digital Club Network

Software: Real Player, Flash.

The Digital Club Network was launched this summer by the team that has held an annual online music 'festival' since 1995. This four-day event started life as the Macintosh New York Festival, bringing together over 300 bands performing – including Bush, Public Enemy, Everlast and Blondie – in seven New York clubs.

Continuously streaming and archiving performances by emerging and established artists from over 30 clubs in seven US cities, the site aims to have a wired network of clubs throughout Europe and Australia by the end of next year. New shows are presented each night, with rebroadcasts and on-demand archives available throughout the day, providing fans with access to previously unavailable live performances 24 hours a day, seven days a week.

The site design is smashing. You surf the funky blue backdrop to even funkier sounds, and pick one of four links to go straight to the current stream, view future schedules or scan the clubs' and bands' archived 'performances'. At the time of writing, all live streams and archived material could be accessed for free, but the company does have plans to start charging, depending on an artist's popularity. This means that some material will be on a pay-per-view basis or paid download. For the time being, the site is funky and free.

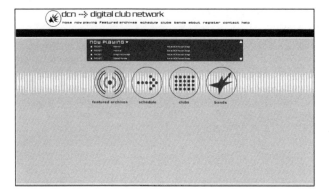

COOL STUFF

• DCN's webcasts include both audio and video streaming, background information on the artists and clubs, and public and private chats. Users are, in theory at least, able to create a virtual chat bar during a particular show to discuss the act. Like meeting a whole bunch of strangers at a gig and having a drink, supposedly.

A superfunky site with beautifuly simple access to streams from some of the hottest New York and Californian clubs.

music

overall rating:	★ ★ ★ ★
classification:	download & streaming source
updated:	weekly
navigation:	★ ★ ★ ★
content:	★ ★ ★
readability:	★ ★ ★
speed:	★ ★ ★ ★
US	

http://www.mp3.com
MP3

Software: Realplayer.

Since its launch in 1998, MP3.com has become synonymous with the birthing pains of the online music revolution. Its founder, Michael Robertson, has become, initially unwittingly, the figurehead for the movement towards entirely different ways of accessing and interacting with music and artists. Depending on which side you're on, he's either the destroyer of the music industry or a crusading hero.

The site was originally designed as a showcase resource for unsigned musicians; where music could be posted in MP3 format free of charge. Lately, it has become more involved with offering mainstream, signed artists. In early 2000 the company began offering a service which allowed users to digitise their music collections and new CD purchases for storage online. Dubbed My.MP3.com, the service was shut down a couple of months later, following court action by the major record labels. It has since obtained royalty licences with three labels – Warner, EMI and BMG – to legally digitise their artists' music, but has yet to reach agreements with Universal and Sony, or any of the music publishers, so the service is still fairly limited.

Despite its varying quality (the majority of radio programming on the stations channel is created by bored amateurs), the breadth and depth of music on the site, both from unsigned and self-published artists, ensures that it is a must for discovering new music. A simple AltaVista-style-interface makes for easy navigation, and the site as a whole is a superb starting point for cybersonic newbies.

COOL STUFF

• The Beam-it download is designed to instantly recognise your CD music collection (via the CD drive) and provide a digitised version in the My.MP3 locker, which you must first register for. Nice idea if you want an electronic version of your existing music collection and don't want to spend hours ripping and encoding.

• The instant listening feature automatically creates a digital copy of CDs bought online (in your My.MP3.com locker), provided you buy from an affiliated retailer, and that artist's label is licensed.

• The Getting Started pages explain the deal with listening to MP3s and how to navigate the hundreds of pages on the site.

• MP3.com offers more than a quarter of a million songs from over 50,000 artists, which are available for free downloading. They occasionally have free stuff from established artists, too. Previously, these included Alanis Morissette, Tori Amos, Beastie Boys, Billy Idol, Tina Turner, Pete Townshend, Dionne Warwick, George Clinton and Master P, as well as all the great unsigned.

• The MP3 soft and hardware pages are a genuinely useful resource featuring the latest news and reviews for all on and offline players and formats, with space for user comment.

• MP3.com has become a hub for debate on digital access to music, and you can find some interesting and (sometimes) intelligent discussion on the message boards. Good for getting answers to technical questions, too.

• If you are an aspiring musician, MP3.com offers a fairly good deal, including a free personalised web page, manufacturing of physical formats for sale (50/50 profit split) and even a chance to earn money via the Payback for Playback program. Crucially, all artists featured retain full copyright to their art.

OTHER STUFF

• The News and Views channel brings dispatches from the digital frontline, culled from US sources such as the Washington Post and Inside.com, with links to readers' comments.

Not a great site for finding consistently good music, but a must for MP3 beginners and a worthy source for aspiring artists prepared to do their own marketing in order to ensure that people go to their particular page out of the thousands available on the site.

http://www.radiospy.com
RadioSpy

Software: Realplayer.

RadioSpy is a global aggregator of SHOUTcast, Windows Media and RealAudio streaming audio servers across the web, sorting them by genre, number of listeners and bandwidth. This is a fantastic resource tool for streaming virgins, especially if you've yet to make your choice of player, even if the functional site interface is more reliable than sleek!

To hear the stations through RadioSpy, you must download Winamp and the RadioSpy player, which is specially configured for multi-channel streaming. In addition to its own fairly bland techno, jazz/blues, pop, alt.rock, classical and 1980s channels, there are a massive 46 genre station links on the homepage, with clear indications of required connection speed for each station to avoid buffering and jerky listening. If you think you can do better, and feel ready for your Warholian 15 minutes of fame, RadioSpy has free downloadable DJ tools with which you can quickly and easily set up your own online radio stations.

COOL STUFF

• The search function on the homepage will seek out stations playing a particular artist or genre. Stations are sorted on a variety of criteria, including playlist, how often it features your favourite artists, and how recently they've done so.

overall rating:	★ ★ ★ ★
classification:	streaming sounds & tools
updated:	weekly
navigation:	★ ★ ★ ★
content:	★ ★ ★ ★
readability:	★ ★ ★ ★
speed:	★ ★ ★ ★
US	

music

• A full guide to getting started with the RadioSpy player, and, unusually, a comprehensive decoding of associated terms, such as 'bit rate', in the download channel.

• Once you've entered your favourite songs into the Notify Me! feature, you'll be able to see all the songs as they start on the 'What's Playing Now?' tab. Click any listing and you'll be connected to that station.

OTHER STUFF

• Weekly updated news from across the streaming/download spectrum. Refreshingly, RadioSpy's coverage is intelligent, bang-up-to date and sometimes exclusively ahead of the pack.

• Artist profiles and reviews of new releases from across its musical spectrum, complete with a channel spinning the reviewed tracks.

• Of course, a multi-room chat area, although not with much action, and a forum channel with four general topics linked via the left-hand side menu on the homepage.

A broad streaming aggregator suitable for streaming virgins, with easy-to-use tools for creating your own MP3 station. (There are many sites designed for personal MP3 programing; you could also take a look at Shoutcast.com and mycaster.com).

http://www.soundbreak.com
Soundbreak

Software: Real Player, Flash.

Another web baby, Soundbreak was launched at the beginning of 2000 as a next generation site, primarily to target the new generation of broadband-connected kids. It is essentially an interactive, video radio station designed to promote new leftfield artists, and stands out for its attention to detail and for taking the web radio potential seriously. Soundbreak offers specially designed programming rather than just slapping on a few DJ mixes, and, in return for relinquishing your email address, all content is freely accessed.

The site is skilfully designed, with fun and noisy graphic links to the streaming and chat areas of the site. The only downside is that it has been built with broadband in mind, so weeny little dial-up connections tend not to cope with its whizzing graphic and high bit-rate streams well, despite being able to choose a 28 connection when you log-in. Once you're in, though, it's funky and free, and hosts sessions and interviews with artists such as Ice T, Fatboy Slim and Queen Latifah, as well as lesser-known mortals. One to watch.

COOL STUFF

• The site recently added new shows hosted by legendary West Coast rap artists Greg Mack and Jim Neil.

overall rating:	★ ★ ★ ★
classification:	live audio/visual webcasting
updated:	daily
navigation:	★ ★ ★ ★
content:	★ ★ ★ ★
readability:	★ ★ ★ ★
speed:	★ ★ ★ ★
US	

• The Music of my Life show invites celebrity guests to speak about and play music, from film directors to old rockers like John Taylor of Duran Duran fame.

OTHER STUFF

• You can watch and send emails to the DJ/host during a show, and then watch their reaction.

• Get information about the music playing and choose to buy via the links to the Soundbreak store to the left of the webcast window.

A site which has spotted the potential for broadcasting in an audio-visual format online, and brims with future promise.

OTHER SITES OF INTEREST

Groove Factory
http://www.groovefactory.com
Another West Coast project with an eclectic list of stations which broadcast techno, tech-house, house, downtempo, mushroom, jazz, ambient, progressive house and trance. A pretty pleasant and easily navigated site, it will connect you to relevant streaming sounds from the likes of RadioSpy (see review), LiveDJs.com, the UK's Gatecrasher and Transcendant radio.

eFestivals
http://www.efestivals.co.uk
While we wait for the webcast sites to get the rights and technical stuff together, and for those of us still labouring under the constraints of narrowband connections, efestivals.co.uk saves the day. Packed with popular message boards, exclusive interviews and festival news and photos from all the main events, this basic site is a useful resource for all festival-related information and activities. Claims to be by festival-goers, for Festival-goers, which is nice in its hippyish way.

Transcasts
http://www.transcasts.com
A basic, no-frills site listing links and brief introductions to worldwide sources for online radio, clubcasts, mix sessions and live webcasts around dance genres. It can be hit-and-miss, but

there are some gems, such as the French Dream-escape.org and U2's Kitchen club sounds.

Stream Search

http://www.tss.com

Stream Search does exactly what the name suggests. Like Transcasts, it can be a bit hit-and-miss, but if you simply have to find that remix – it must be on the web somewhere – then Stream Search wouldn't be a bad first port of call. Results are delivered in all formats for both video and audio, and sometimes include downloads as well as streams.

unsigned talent

Scores of dotcoms offering varying deals to unsigned artists to get online exposure have appeared since MP3.com reared its head and began to make waves in mid-1998. Quite a few of them were carried away by the potential to become online publishers or 'labels', and dominate an emerging market for less commendable motives than having a passion for giving the best emerging talent a 'voice', and punters a chance to discover new music outside the realms of mainstream radio and TV. Never fear, the Good Web Guide team has endeavoured to seek out the sites sporting genuinely interesting talent and offering reliable and honest deals for artists. MP3.com continues to offer the best deal for artists (see review in chapter 4), in terms of no-strings-attached hosting, but doesn't offer the same sort of access to industry eyes and ears as some of its competitors. Whether you're an aspiring artist looking for effective exposure, or an enthusiastic talent seeker, we offer the top five.

music

http://www.musicunsigned.com
Music Unsigned

Software: Real Player.

With its strict selection procedure and offline industry experience and contacts, Music Unsigned remains one of the best sites for both featured artists and its visitors. Unlike many unsigned showcase sites, the number of acts is restricted, and each has undergone stringent quality control, so the numbers are kept to a manageable, highly listenable selection.

Strangely, the site has recently transformed from being quite funky and minimal, sticking to the basics of showcasing creamy new talent, to a broader and uglier site which attempts to cover more bases than it needs to. For example, the Festival channel, with its links to all of 2000's main events on the right of the homepage, has no interactive elements. What it does have is badly written and half-finished reviews, which they shouldn't really have bothered with. Likewise, the album and singles reviews are randomly selected, if competently written.

Still, the site's core element of providing a space to hear unsigned bands still exists, in all its glorious simplicity. The acts on the site are divided into seven broad genres: pop, alternative, club, easy, rock, urban and world. These are then subdivided into three: experimental, dance and rock in the alternative genre, for example. However, extra padding has been added in an attempt to compete with broader UK music portals, with, it must be said, a few unnecessary misses such as the festival and culture coverage. That said, a few of the added features, such as the Blue List, business-to-business directory and the news coverage, are useful winners.

On the artist side, the site appears to have ditched its original contractual obligations, as prospective artists can submit music directly for free via the simple online sign-up form. Free is good, but the crucial issue of copyright ownership once an act is accepted and posted on the site does not seem to merit a mention. We'd suggest that any hopefuls should check this out thoroughly before signing on the dotted line, especially as the site has recently formed its own label and publishing arm.

COOL STUFF

• A variety of interesting news and gossip from the alternative mainstream and independent outposts.

• The Blue List, accessible via the left homepage menu, is a free and exhaustive database of UK business contacts for everything from media to advertising agencies to retailers. Nice touch.

OTHER STUFF

• Unsigned acts can advertise their gigs on the gig list page, and users are invited to send in reviews of live acts for consideration.

music

• Extensive features from the upcoming talent frontline, from Daft Punk protégés Modjo, to ex-Stone Roses frontman Ian Brown's emerging solo efforts.

• Songlocation.com, linked via the Music Unsigned homepage, is a forthcoming 'service' which aims to provide a database of screened signed and unsigned music for use by business interests such as advertising executives and A&R men.

• The Undercurrent pages in the Features section, linked via the right-hand channel on the homepage, are reserved for features and reviews on newly signed buzz acts, along with details of where to see them playing. Be in on the industry buzz before it happens, according to Music Unsigned's judgement.

• The sample police page in the features section attempts to be a humourous undressing of uncredited pillaging of classics by artists that should know better. It's fairly amusing, if you've got nothing better to do.

Though the central elements of this site are almost buried in a mass of badly constructed contents, you won't be displeased with what you find.

http://www.popwire.com

Popwire

Software: QuickTime.

Having racked up 11 label signings for its acts with a variety of British, Swedish and US independent labels, Popwire is probably the best of the unsigned bunch. Acting as an industry search engine and 'pop star incubator', popwire.com appears to be serious about the business of building the potential for musicians to become established artists, as well as helping the industry to identify new and profitable stars.

Like Musicunsigned, Popwire exercises stringent vetting of material before unleashing it on its audience, resulting in a smoother and realistic sonic surf of the great unknown than catch-all garage band sites such as MP3.com. Aside from showcasing exciting new talent, Popwire offers a variety of well-designed, well-thought-out added-value music information tools, such as the pan-national gig listings and the sublime news, reviews and gossip ezine.

From an aspiring artist's point of view, if your material gets accepted by the Popwire team, which include a variety of seasoned music and internet professionals, and freely posted on the site, you should have a greater chance of achieving some sort of notice. The Popwire top 25 weekly chart lists the most downloaded tracks, letting you know instantly if you're onto a winner! It's worth noting that all artists showcased by Popwire

| overall rating: |
| ★ ★ ★ ★ ★ |
| classification: |
| emerging talent site |
| updated: |
| weekly |
| navigation: |
| ★ ★ ★ ★ ★ |
| content: |
| ★ ★ ★ ★ |
| readability: |
| ★ ★ ★ ★ |
| speed: |
| ★ ★ ★ ★ ★ |
| SWE |

take on publishing rights. Popwire artists are accessible on the site via 17 broad genres, including country, drum'n'bass, classical and alternative.

COOL STUFF

• Popwire's monthly magazine is a real online glossy. Accessible via the media channel, the magazine combines true online design style with cutting edge editorial to deliver some informative features, reviews, gossip, gigs and news from the Popwire artist frontline as well as on more established artists, such as Beverly Knight. The title can also be downloaded and printed in PDF format, to relieve those tired eyes. The gig listings are definitely worth a look too, with upcoming bands listed nationwide, Europe-wide and for some US dates.

• The Popwire TV webcasts weekly shows of unsigned buzz gigs across Europe. This means you can watch as well as listen, which makes the site nearly unique among its competitors.

• Informative news and features on upcoming releases, collaborations, gossip and gigs from Popwire artists and established pan-European acts.

• The MP3 tools channel is a fantastic and extensive resource guide for players, divided into platform compatibility and complete with both no-nonsense reviews and download links.

• Find out who's hot in the weekly updated Popwire top 25 downloaded tracks, complete with indications of fastest climber and highest new entry.

• Multilingual; it can be viewed in Japanese and Spanish as well as English.

• Popwire radio spins the best of its artists via three channels – pop, harder and urban – which are accessible via the Popwire Media channel.

A rich, sassy, effective and interactive pan-European resource for sampling emerging talent, in addition to comprehensive news, features and gig information from the alternative independent frontline.

music

overall rating:	★★★★
classification:	new talent showcase site
updated:	weekly
navigation:	★★★★
content:	★★★★
readability:	★★★★
speed:	★★★★
UK	

http://www.btgetoutthere.com

British Telecom

Software: Beatnik Player.

At first glance you may be forgiven for wondering what British Telecom is doing. Are they trying to get down with the kids? It's a good question, and BT would be open to much ridicule if the site failed to impress. However, BT's GetOutThere team have created a slick, highly interactive, good-looking and fun site, with some real incentives for sharing your music.

This is a site for DJ/producer wannabes, not professionals, and it isn't really meant for the casual visitor either. Viewed cynically, it's ultimately designed to collect email addresses, but at least it provides a solid incentive to get involved and play around. The interface is smooth and easily navigated, and it keeps the content within frames on one page to save you from getting lost in a jungle of pages. There are some natty graphics too, and pretty cool prizes to be won by whoever submits the best mixes. All good, clean, teenage bedroom DJ fun.

COOL STUFF

• The studio pages within the music channel includes a virtual remix room where you can try your skills at remixing some kindly donated Freestyler and Laurent Nelson tracks; the Cuts & Beats section lets you play around with vocal samples to the tune of several Freestylers loops, and the drum machine section is a virtual and interactive, well, drum machine. This section also lists extensive links to freeware music production tools sites and hosts a technical Q&A forum.

• All music showcased on the site is charted by number of downloads, compiled monthly and accessible via the music channel. All entries are hyperlinked for audio clips. The chart is weighted to favour sites getting recent downloads, not just numbers. It also claims to be fix-proof.

• Top ten uploaded tracks are judged by different DJs each month, from Tall Paul to Roger Sanchez. Winning entries receive equipment, club tickets and recognition but sadly, there are no record deals on offer.

• The silent video competition involves a video download to which you must compose a soundtrack and upload again to enter. Independent film producers judge submissions and winners are shown on Kiss TV and the Box. This is a nice idea, and possibly good practice for real beginners.

OTHER STUFF

• The site has put together a full, fledgling DJ/producer channel on how to get ahead in – you guessed it – the White Island. The Day by Day is mostly frivolous banter about where to be seen, but does have a couple of phone numbers and details of DJ competitions and places to meet other DJs. If you want it that badly, here it is.

• Read articles on how current DJ darlings made it to superstar status, and get their advice on starting up in the Musical Express channel. Light and fluffy as this is, it's a nice touch. This channel also includes a minimal gig guide, features on emerging artists and a buy-and-sell message board for equipment and instruments. It's hard to tell how effective this latter is, though, as there are several messages that are months old.

• The Contests channel includes a number of competitions around creating samples and beats, music trivia quizzes to win VIP tickets to gigs and clubs, to meet real live pop stars.

A fun site aimed at getting cool with generation Y bedroom DJs.

http://www.peoplesound.com

Peoplesound

Software: Realplayer

Peoplesound has tried hard to be fresh, funky and down with
the kids ever since its launch back in the summer of 1999. After
a few false starts due to being over ambitious with its
technology – the site can be slow to load its pages –
Peoplesound largely fulfils its ambition to appeal to the net-
savvy sonic surfer. The design is hip and the interface clean,
concise and easily navigated, although some of the pages don't
always load properly on first click. The material on Peoplesound
is divided into 16 genres – including urban, rock, reggae and
classical – which are then subdivided into up to eight sections.
The majority of the artists featured are unsigned, although you
will find some independent labels' emerging artists featured;
think Helicopter Girl and Attica Blues. Thankfully, the material is
also screened by an army of A&R footsoldiers across its
European territories.

From an artist's point of view, the emphasis is on the site finding
you, rather than you finding them, although all material sent is
considered. Unlike other unsigned sites, you must send in a CD
for consideration, rather than simply uploading your material. If
you get accepted, you will be paid £100, for which you will be
asked to sign away your online publishing rights. Where this
site really excels on behalf of fledgling artists is in its extensive,
informed advice and genuinely amusing, informed articles on

overall rating:
★ ★ ★ ★
classification:
unsigned showcase/fledgling label
updated:
weekly
navigation:
★ ★ ★
content:
★ ★ ★ ★
readability:
★ ★ ★ ★
speed:
★ ★ ★
IT

every aspect of the music business, from organising your press and promotion to dealing with groupies. All such material can be found in the artist support channel.

COOL STUFF

• Peoplesound deserve credit for coming up with an impressive new way to search out music. Simply select the Search by Mood link on the homepage, fill in your favourite artists and you will be presented with a selection of available artists deemed by the software to suit your tastes, whether you want to listen in the bath, get ready to go out or dig out a suitable musical backdrop to essay-writing, among others. Neat.

• In return for surrendering that email address you will be the proud recipient of a CD featuring the best of Peoplesound's material.

• None other than Judge Jules himself – boy, does he get around online these days – compiles a weekly pick of the Peoplesound top five dance tracks. Read the ruling and follow the listen links.

• The site has recently diversified into hawking a menagerie of electronic music equipment, including everything from mixing desks to state-of-the-art samplers at up to half the recommended retail price. You can find these in the Digital Village channel.

OTHER STUFF

• Peoplesound often runs easy competitions in the offers channel, with some pretty funky prizes such as an MP3 Casio watch. Be prepared to part with that email address and profile, though.

• View the top 20 downloads in the chart channel, complete with a brief description of each track and listening links.

• The Music Alert monthly email will send updates of new material on the site, according to your stated preferences.

• The editorial and A&R teams compile their choice of top 10 tracks on the site each week. You can find these in the editors' choice channel.

• If you're a regular visitor to the site, you can check out the daily updated, freshly added material in the Latest Arrivals channel.

• If you like what you hear, you can choose from six Peoplesound compilation CD titles, on the compilation channels.

An achingly hip, serious stab at creating an online platform for screened emerging talent. Nice to look at, interesting to listen to.

music

overall rating:	★ ★ ★ ★
classification:	unsigned showcase/fledgling label
updated:	weekly
navigation:	★ ★ ★ ★
content:	★ ★ ★ ★ ★
readability:	★ ★ ★
speed:	★ ★ ★ ★ ★
IT	

http://www.vitaminic.com
Vitaminic

Software: Realplayer.

Set up as a local talent site by a group of passionate Italians last summer, Vitaminic has rapidly expanded to sites in six European countries – including the UK – and the US. The site's interface is far from sexy, with the company preferring to focus on speed, functionality and depth of content, both in terms of music and comprehensive guides on getting started with MP3 downloading and streaming. This site, therefore is an excellent launch pad for sonicsurf virgins. There are no obvious 'success' stories to date, at least in terms of artists winning recording contracts through exposure on the site, although that isn't always the ultimate aim of all aspiring musicians! Not being musicians ourselves, it's hard to gauge whether Vitaminic is the best choice for success. However, it does offer no-strings-attached hosting of your music and a chance to get out there.

Vitaminic provides free download and streaming access to thousands of MP3 files, across 150 genres, by both unsigned artists and more established ones, who have chosen to use the site to gain extra awareness for their music. These are usually fringe acts that have more control over their own promotion. Unlike some of its competitors, Vitaminic will post most music submitted to its site (albeit with light screening) and makes no claims to own any sort of copyright to your music once you enter the free, open-ended contract.

COOL STUFF

• Vitaminic is, if nothing else, committed to educating users about the what, where and how of MP3. The topics in the All About MP3 section cover the basics, from what an MP3 is and a full guide to downloading, to whether your PC/Mac is equipped to properly experience online audio. It also gives the lowdown on MP3 hard and software players. A must-see for beginners.

• The site gives some attention to the crucial areas of copyright issues around MP3 and has included a comprehensive FAQ on this area. Other topics within the FAQ include details about the artist contract, questions about the Vitaminic site and its policy, and questions around general MP3 basics.

• Up to 220 street labels throughout Europe and the US are detailed in the Labels channel, some with links to their material and links to their own sites where available.

• The gig listings channel lists many major artists currently touring in the UK, with hyperlinks to ticket hotlines, venues and other relevant information.

Each channel has an affiliated radio station which will pop up in a separate window if you click on the obvious hyperlink in each channel. The station's content consists of random programming of tracks on the site, which could be useful if you haven't the patience to download lots of individual tracks or if you want to test the quality of the content on the site.

OTHER STUFF

• Like most sites, Vitaminic encourages you to sign up for the weekly email update of all that's new at the site and in the world of MP3 beyond. Vitaminic news isn't included on the site.

• Each genre has a top 10 download chart.

A basic, fully-functioning, no-frills site designed to give exposure to emerging pan-European and US talent. With its comprehensive MP3 starter-kit guides, Vitaminic is a useful resource for sonic surf virgins.

fans

One of the main effects of the birth of the internet has been empowerment. Anybody with access to the internet can design their own homepage for free and put whatever they like on it. While this is great for freedom of speech, a great deal of personal homepages aren't worth the visit. However, there are some fantastic sites in cyberspace published by supa-fans with probably too much time on their hands and too much devotion.

This chapter includes the most innovative, beautiful, and interactive official artist sites, useful artist network portals, and of course, examples of the best fan sites. We have also included links to all the nation's favourite artists. This section could never be exhaustive by any means. Therefore, if you can't find a link here, the Good Web Guide team recommend the following search engines: www.ubl.com, www.clickmusic.co.uk, www.musicfans.com, and www.yahoo.com. Or try www.fansites.com, top.mosiqa.com, or www.musicfansites.com. There are also many fanclubs online offering the latest news, links to loads of sites, and chat; two of the best are www.clubs.yahoo.com and www.vh1.com/fanclubs.

portals

It would be impossible to compile a list of artist websites that satisfied everyone. If you are desperate to find the website of your favourite band and they're not listed in this chapter, try one of these portals; they have links to thousands of artists, and with a bit of luck, it will include the one you're looking for.

www.musicfans.com
Musicfans

overall rating:
★ ★ ★ ★ ★
classification:
unofficial fan site network
updated:
weekly
navigation:
★ ★ ★ ★
content:
★ ★ ★ ★
readability:
★ ★ ★ ★ ★
speed:
★ ★ ★ ★ ★
US

Although Musicfans was founded in 1999, it is still very much in the process of building its network of the best global unofficial fan sites across all genres. This site is apparently created by music fans for music fans, and is basically doing the scouring, getting stuck in black holes, and plucking out the shiny webjewels so that you don't have to, which is nice.

The site is well designed for easy navigation, with functional interface. It currently has around 100 unofficial sites listed for bands such as U2 and Radiohead, with the emphasis on depth rather than breadth of content. Although Musicfans is backed by a corporate team, they have actually realised that the real value of the net is about creating strong communities, and are building a business on providing a destination where all kinds of music fans will find links to the best sites – built by fans – that truly represent their interests. Its about bringing together like-minded people to share ideas, thoughts, and useful information, and that's the real reason why the web is so cool.

COOL STUFF

• Each site listing links you to a pop-up window with a short but informative précis of what the site has to offer, including a link to the actual site, which opens in a separate window, so you can get back to Musicfans without any fuss.

music

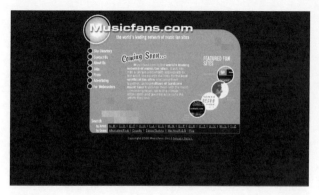

• Musicfans is constantly on the look out for new sites to add to its database, so if you think your fan site is cooler than most, send in your details.

A fantastic resource for finding the best unofficial fan and genre sites for all tastes, Musicfans takes the sting out of the minefield of visiting numerous duff official sites or lame homepages by pointing you to the real gems.

www.artistdirect.com
Artist Direct Network

software: Real Player

The Artist Direct Network is pretty bland in terms of presentation and depth of content, but it's the extent of artist information on its Ultimate Band List and iMusic sister sites which makes it a useful first-stop resource for finding official and unofficial links to a wide spectrum of artists. The Artist Direct destination is itself focused on building shopfronts for artists and selling physical music formats and merchandise. Although the site is uninspired, if you missed out on that must-have tour shirt, then this is your show, baby. The Network's real treasures, however, lie in the UBL and iMusic; in both the emphasis is on functionality rather than beauty. These sites aren't going to win any design awards, but if you need to find an artist fast, the UBL is always a safe first click for the browser, using a simple search engine function on the homepage, and it packs some useful links listings to radio and other music resource sites. iMusic claims to be the largest music community online. The largest doesn't always mean the best, but again, if you're looking for first-stop information, artist chat, and messageboards, this site is worth a look.

A first-stop resource for tracking down artist information online. Use it and leave.

overall rating:
★ ★ ★

classification:
artist network

updated:
occasionally

navigation:
★ ★ ★ ★

content:
★ ★ ★ ★

readability:
★ ★ ★ ★ ★

speed:
★ ★ ★ ★ ★

UK

best artist sites

These sites form a small selection of the best designed and technically executed on the internet. They are included to show what fan sites (official or unofficial) should be like. So, even if you're not a fan, they might be worth checking out. If you are a devoted fan and want to set up a website, then these sites will give you some idea of what to aspire to.

www.intimate.org/bjork

Bjork −The Ultimate Intimate

Put together by an oddball Icelandic collective of web designers and journalists, this site is widely regarded as the best place for all Bjork information and music. Spanning her entire career − from fronting the Sugarcubes to her recent starring role in Dancer in the Dark − the Ultimate Intimate is an exhaustive, fairly easily navigated, and competently designed site, which isn't afraid to share her music for free too. The only omission is the lack of message boards or chatrooms. The best feature of the site is its proximity to the artist, meaning it often has new release and tour news before any other media source, including the official site at www.bjork.com.

overall rating:
★ ★ ★ ★ ★
classification:
unofficial fan site
updated:
weekly
navigation:
★ ★ ★
content:
★ ★ ★ ★
readability:
★ ★ ★ ★ ★
speed:
★ ★ ★ ★ ★
US

COOL STUFF

• The discography channel, 77 Island, linked via the right-hand menu on the homepage, contains pages related to all periods of Bjork's career, from the Sugarcubes, through to Dancer in the Dark. Exhaustive.

• The Quotes/FAQ channel contains the singer's musings on everything, from feminism, to love and quotes from other artists. Interesting for the devoted fan.

• The video, audio, and remixriot pages have extensive free streams and downloads which span the artist's career.

• Users can subscribe to the Bjork community mailing list to get the very latest information on tours, collaborations, and releases on the Blue Eyed Pop channel. The mailing list also carries information on other up-and-coming Icelandic artists.

OTHER STUFF

• The News Archive pages have all the latest info on the Icelandic princess, from her movie appearances, to tours, to new music (the schedule section has details of all releases in the past year and any current tour information).

• The Bootography channel has links to all bootlegged CDs produced from her TV and live performances ... Maybe a little dodgy?

• The Gigography channel lists all gigs of the singer's solo career, and the Lyrics channel has all her lyrics (both solo and with the Sugarcubes).

• The Pictures channel has downloadable pix of the star from childhood to her Cannes appearances.

• View fan art and send in your own on the Art Gallery channel

• The Specials channel has links to pages with miscellaneous features such as articles, logs of Bjork's online chat, and her April Fools Jokes. Can you know too much?

• The Guestbook is where you can share your love for Bjork and the site ...

A comprehensive and solid resource and probably the most reliable destination for the latest information and audio links for the Sugarcubes and Bjork.

music

www.blur.org.uk
Blurred For Life

Software: Realplayer and Quicktime.

Blurred For Life is a suitably hip site catering for all possible information, sounds, and interactive needs of any admirers of the superstar Colchester Crew. Blurred is a real labour of love – you'll find pages and pages of sublimely presented articles and flash games, as well as all of Blur's music and Coxon's solo music in stream, MP3 download, and Midi formats. There are also hundreds of webcast interviews, live gigs, and official videos, and a sophisticated internationally-populated chat and message board area. Blurred For Lifers are a dedicated lot and honour the site with their daily devotion, creating a true, if irregularly updated online community. Containing many exclusive links to live footage and pre-release material, this site is probably the best unofficial fan site in cyberspace.

COOL STUFF

• The site has recently launched a nattily designed ezine called Five Fingers. Click the link on the homepage, and follow the picture links to well-written, informative articles about the group's recent activities, a b-style section about where to get hold of the clothes and accessories the group favour (only for the seriously devoted), A Who Are Ya page dedicated to fans, and competitions.

• Listen to exclusive streams and get MP3 and midi downloads of new Blur material pre-release and a full list of all Blur tracks and remixes on the Sounds channel, linked via the main drop-down menu on the front page. Supa!

• The Videos channel has an incredible selection of all of Blur's single videos and webcast interviews with the band, plus some exclusive footage.

• The Blur chatroom is populated by a really friendly, chatty crowd with an international flava. The Coping channel is the incredibly extensive and active messageboards, which seem to be another line of communication for all those sexy Blur chatroom cats.

• The Multimedia channel has some wallpaper sounds and graphix for the Blurriest 'puter on the block, plus some really cool little Flash games.

• Send a Blur epostcard to your fellow Blurophiles on the Postcards channel, funnily enough.

OTHERSTUFF

• The Newspage features the (nearly) latest tour and release news.

• Save embarrassing yourself Garth-style at the next gig and learn the lyrics off by heart on the Lyrics channel.

music

- Brush-up on your Blur knowledge in the full discography and biography section.

- Make Blurette buddies via the Blur mailing list.

- The not-so-long Links page (Blurred For Life wants you to stick around) includes links to Blur's label site and official fanclub site among others.

An incredibly stylish and wonderfully rich multimedia resource that does the Blurheads proud.

www.brainwashed.com

Brainwashed

Software: Real Player, Microsoft Media.

Brainwashed started life in the mid-nineties as an online presence for post-modern electro beats fringers Meat Beat Manifesto. It has since metamorphosed into a non-profit network hosting sites for artists as diverse as Cabaret Volitaire and Bomb The Bass. It is information-orientated, simple to navigate, and very easy on the eye. Claiming to serve no other purpose than the exchange of music and information, the site shuns outside advertising of any kind. The music page has links to over 50 artist sites – hosted within the Brainwashed frame – with audio clips and all the usual news and discography information, in addition to a mailing list, and chat and forum links. The Stores page is a useful links reference for hard-to-find physical mail order resources and definitely worth a look.

overall rating:	
★ ★ ★ ★ ★	
classification:	
artist network and label site	
updated:	
occasionally	
navigation:	
★ ★ ★ ★	
content:	
★ ★ ★ ★	
readability:	
★ ★ ★ ★ ★	
speed:	
★ ★ ★ ★ ★	
US	

COOL STUFF

• Many of the artist sites have up-to-the-minute downloadable MP3 track clips from much of their catalogue, most of which you'd be hard-pushed to find anywhere else online – even on Napster. You can get a full round-up of MP3s from all the artists on the Brainwashed Jukebox page on the Music channel.

• Brainwashed hosts the complete Axis resources online, subliminal and epochal art, music and literature, and socio-political anarchist media movement, accessed via the Music channel.

• Updates of new releases and tour news from all the artists hosted on the site, can be found on The Brain channel via the Music page.

• Browse and buy Brainwashed's own vinyl/CD efforts through the Brainwashed Recordings channel on the Music channel, and selected independent labels' stuff, hosted by the site, through the label links in the same place.

• Get t-shirts, and selected CDs, on the Merchandise Channel.

• The Stores channel has links to online mail-order music stores across the UK, Europe, and the US, revealing such gems as Chunky (http://www.users.globalnet.co.uk/~chunkymo/) and Rocket Girl Records (http://www.rocketgirl.demon.co.uk/).

OTHER STUFF

• Each artist site has links to the label, fans' sites, and mailing lists, and many have full news, discography, reviews, history pages, and email contact details.

• Find out who makes it happen on the People pages which come complete with email addresses.

This is reputedly the best site of its kind, and is an exemplary resource with great art, links and merchandise.

www.greenplastic.com

Greenplastic – Radiohead

Software: Realplayer and Quicktime.

Greenplastic is a longstanding, ever-involving uberfan site of a rare quality, both in terms of information and presentation; a site of which the increasingly web-friendly Radiohead would probably be proud.

Painstakingly put together, this slick, deep tour through everything Radiohead contains page after sublime page of everything from tour info through to philosophical musings from one of the UK's most interesting current rock bands. Radiohead have increasingly embraced the web as their preferred means of communicating with their fans, and are one of the rare established bands who see the benefits of the medium rather than kicking against it in Metallica-esque style.

As a result, this site, with its streaming audio and refusal to trade in MP3s, and its pure style and dedication to the phenomenon of the band is a must-visit cyberspace destination for any fan of the Oxford quartet. All channels and related pages are simply navigated via the hyperlink menu on the homepage, and community messageboards are thriving. There is also plenty of opportunity for fans to submit examples of their love by contributing to song interpretations, and submitting their artwork and reviews.

overall rating:	★ ★ ★ ★ ★
classification:	unofficial fan site
updated:	weekly
navigation:	★ ★ ★
content:	★ ★ ★ ★ ★
readability:	★ ★ ★ ★
speed:	★ ★ ★ ★ ★
US	

COOL STUFF

• Greenplastic's News and Rumours pages round up all reports and hearsay published about the band on the internet, complete with links. Saves trawling. Nice.

• The audio page on the Multimedia channel has streaming access to much of Radiohead's live repertoire. You can't download MP3 files here, out of respect for the band, although there is a link elsewhere enabling you to do so.

• The Multimedia channel also has extensive lists of Radiohead videos and interviews, which can be watched via streaming through Real Play or Quicktime.

• Get a full list of international tour information and links to ticket outlets on the Tour Dates page. You can also link to text and graphics from previous tours via this page.

• A simple, graphic chronology of the band is beautifully presented on the Chronology page. Nice touch.

• Another little gem lies within the Philosophical channel. Memorise the band's thoughts on life, collected from across the web, magazine interviews, etc., and claim them as your own in order to impress your mates ...

• The Shop page contains links to the best sources for getting hold of Radiohead merchandise online, including a link to W.A.S.T.E, the band's official store.

OTHER STUFF

• Get the full lowdown on the history of the band and its individual members on the Band Info pages.

• The Discography channel has pages detailing complete track listings, and review information for every Radiohead single, album, collaboration, and video release.

• Get complete lyrics and song information for all tracks on the Lyrics channel.

• Find an exhaustive band photo library on the Multimedia Channel, where you can also access pretty funky wallpaper, skins, fonts, and screensaver downloads.

• The Lounge channel lists links to the best chat and messageboards populated by Radiohead fans online, complete with descriptions. Greenplastic has its own messageboard and was about to launch its own chatroom at the time of writing.

• The Gigography pages are just that; a full list of live gigs and webcasts, complete with links to reviews.

• The Oxford Guide page is designed as an introduction to the band's home town; more for US visitors, and possibly verging on the superfluous.

• A full hyperlink list of articles written on the band throughout its history resides on the Articles page.

• Want to play Radiohead? Visit Greenplastic's Tabs channel for hyperlinks to guitar tabs for every track.

• Radiohead fans are an arty bunch, and you can find their pictorial musings on the Artwork channel. Submit your own as well, if you like.

• The Song Interpretations channel is a space for fans to share their ideas about Radiohead's music and what it means. Only for the truly devoted.

• The Links page lists the best of alternative Radiohead sources online.

This superb fan site is one of the best-designed and info-packed on the web, and rivals many official sites. A must for any self-respecting Radiohead fan.

www.jeepster.com

Jeepster

Following the link-up with independent label distributor iCrunch (www.iCrunch.com), the Jeepster label (home of Belle & Sebastian, The Gentle Waves, Looper, Salako, and Snow Patrol) has quickly built up a comprehensive, well-designed and funky site. Easily navigated via a concise menu, the interface is bright, busy, and ultimately sticky. You'll find all the usual features, but it's the well-thought-out extras that make this site worth a visit. Music online should be an interactive experience, rather than a dead-end presentation and user interface, and Jeepster seem to have got this right. The message boards, and especially the chatrooms, have grown amazingly fast to become some of the most popular, fun, and well-populated stations on the sonic surf. The main advantage of the partnership with iCrunch is that you can buy any Jeepster material as digital downloads, as well as being able to listen to the usual 30-second clips.

overall rating:
★ ★ ★ ★ ★
classification:
official label site
updated:
weekly
navigation:
★ ★ ★ ★
content:
★ ★ ★ ★ ★
readability:
★ ★ ★ ★
speed:
★ ★ ★ ★ ★
UK

COOL STUFF

• All of the Jeepster catalogue is available for purchase as digital downloads. Click on the Digital Downloads channel to get there.

• The B&S section has a meet-up board for organising fan picnics and get-togethers, which are fast becoming legendary !

• Each min-site has a fridge magnet section so you can create your own poems, and a graphic story board for fans to test their literary skills. Especially nice touch.

• All Jeepster physical formats can be ordered secure online. Visit the Jeepster Store channel with the plastic.

• Each artist has their own page on the site, with channels for ecommerce, wallpaper, chat, news, message boards, and much more. View a complete discography, listen to clips, and choose to buy some downloads or CDs , or chat to fellow fans. Also featured here are links to the artists' own sites.

OTHER STUFF

• The News pages contain news on all the label's artists. You can find out more about the label on the History and Staff pages, and find out where you can get hold of Jeepster music on the Distributors pages.

• Send Belle & Sebastian or Snow Patrol virtual postcards from the Virtual Postcards pages.

• Fill in your precious email address on the homepage to get email updates on all Jeepster news.

A slick, bright, and busy site providing information and catering for all the interactive needs of fans of the Jeepster artists. A veritable cuddly community.

www.madonnaland.com

Madonnaland

The Material Girl is, as you can probably imagine, represented on the net a thousand times over, but few could rival this site in terms of exhaustive content. This is a Wonderland of facts, stories, photos, music videos, sound clips, FAQs, and awards, all relating to the Detroit-born Madonna. Competently-designed and fairly easy to navigate, Madonnaland is a comprehensive unofficial site dedicated to the dance pop queen, with almost everything you could possibly want , although it has yet to add any music clips, downloads or webcasts. Because of her mass international appeal, Madonna has become one of the most bootlegged artists on the net. The official release date of her single 'Music' was brought forward by two months because it was leaked on to the web, and consequently swapped like wildfire on Napster. Madonna has since spoken out against online 'piracy', and has yet to sanction official promotional MP3s online.

overall rating:
★ ★ ★ ★ ★

classification:
unofficial fan site

updated:
weekly

navigation:
★ ★ ★ ★

content:
★ ★ ★ ★ ★

readability:
★ ★ ★ ★

speed:
★ ★

US

COOL STUFF

• The Forum is an essential for the ultimate fan-community experience as it is broad, informative, and well-populated. Swap devotion stories, and debate Maddy's new album.

• Ever wondered what the hell she was going on about in La Isla Bonita? Find the full lyrics to every track ever recorded on the lyrics page. Print them off to sing from.

• FAQ features anything you ever wanted to know about Madonna; from the films she's starred in to her lovelife, it's all here in one of the most exhaustive biographies on the web.

• A full photo library, divided into pages for family, friends, and official photos. Please note that parental guidance is recommended as the full 'Sex' book photos are included.

• The Fan Creations channel is a space for you to send in your drawings, lyrics, and costume suggestions!

OTHER STUFF

• The M's Music page lists details of every single, album, EP, and video release ever to emerge from the Material Girl's empire. No links to online audio here though.

• Clear up that row about how successful True Blue really was with the full listing of releases, where they charted in the US and the UK, and how many sales the record drummed up internationally, on the Albums and Singles Info pages.

• The Tour Info pages contain exhaustive information on every Madonna tour since the early nineties, with details of complete dates, songs performed, themes, costumes, and additional tour anecdotes (such as when she held up traffic when jogging on the streets of Toronto). These guys are totally devoted. Ditto for her full film appearance history and awards. Lordy!

The creator of this site truly believes that Madonna-love makes the world go round. A must for all devoted fans of the Candy Perfume Girl.

OTHER MADONNA SITES OF INTEREST

Sindri's Madonna Page
www.SindrisMadonnapage.com
Original design, beautiful graphics and archives of Madonna articles.

MLVC.org
www.mlvc.org
Official mailing lists and the mp3s and links in the Girlie channel.

ICON Official Madonna Fan Club
www.madonnafans.com
Madonna's official webpage.

music

overall rating:
★ ★ ★ ★ ★
classification:
official fan site
updated:
weekly
navigation:
★ ★ ★
content:
★ ★ ★ ★ ★
readability:
★ ★ ★ ★
speed:
★ ★ ★ ★ ★
US

www.npgonlineltd.com
Prince

Software: Real Media, Microsoft Media.

Since his infamous tussle with his record label, and consequent departure, Prince has made the web his spiritual home. As well as being a front for his Paisley Park studio and NPG merchandising business, this slick, Flash-heavy cyberspace station is a backdrop for his protest, poetry, and essays on how the world should be. The Artist has plenty to say on freedom of distribution and promotion, and especially expression on and offline, all set out in visually- stimulating environments. Most of the opinions are in real audio format, and some of the poetry is in text-video. Worth a look for desiring critics, and, of course, a must for diehard admirers of the man who made rain purple.

COOL STUFF

• Stream or download a range of the little man's music from his entire career, some full-length, some snippets, on the Groovez channel, and check-out some tacky wallpaper and video clips on the Visualz channel.

• The 1800 NewFunk link to the bottom right of the homepage links through to the NPG store, while the Love4oneanother link takes you to a download page where you can watch Prince's visual poetry on the destructive relationship between Art and Society in a secular world ... Lordy. Only for the real lovers of the post-Symbol icon.

OTHER STUFF

• Read up on the parties at Paisley Park, the latest Prince reviews, and all other NPG news, Prince rants and Q&As, on the Newz channel.

• The Freedom channel is a cornucopia of real audio musings from the likes of George Clinton and Lenny Kravitz, books, music and film recommendations, and other juicy tidbits if you're a like- minded individual.

• Scroll through a picturebook Prince discography on the corresponding channel linked via the round discs to the bottom left of the homepage.

The embittered eighties icon has adopted the web as his spiritual home after rejecting his label and traditional ways of communicating with his fans. A true, slick Prince pastiche paradise for diehard admirers.

music

overall rating:
★ ★ ★ ★ ★

classification:
official artist site

updated:
irregularly

navigation:
★ ★ ★ ★

content:
★ ★ ★ ★

readability:
★ ★ ★ ★

speed:
★ ★ ★

US

www.williamorbit.com
William Orbit

Software: Real Media, Microsoft Media.

The official site for the uber-producer William Orbit (Madonna, Blur, All Saints) would have been a disappointment, not to mention a disservice, if it was anything less than a slick sonic-surf station. The long-standing site doesn't disappoint, and is probably one of the most comprehensive, well-thought out and smooth official artist sites on the web. Along with the exhaustive articles, reviews, discography, and chronology information you would expect, the site sports an audio and video channel of amazing quality, spanning much of the O's work in audio and video form, plus interviews and awards

ceremonies. A soothing backing track (which can be turned off) accompanies the smooth blue, easily-navigated interface, with each of the 12 channels linked through a constant left-hand menu frame. Along with the audio/visual content, the site also hosts an email forum for all Orbit lovers to unite across the globe on a daily basis. Interactive, ingenuous, and irresistible for fans of Orbit from his early work with Sting in the eighties to his Grammy Award-winning work with Madonna in 1998.Though you can't currently buy anything from the site, there are plenty of links on the Store page.

COOL STUFF

• The audio video library has a vast selection of audio clips spanning Orbit's work, available to stream in Real or to download as an MP3 for playback with any player, and videos spanning his artists, interviews, and even Grammy Award ceremonies – available to stream with Real or Windows Media players.

• You can sift through the O's massive musical history on the Discography channel – from 1983 to the present day – broken down by artist, complete with full track listings and availability details.

• The Mailing List page also includes instructions on how to join the email forum populated by Orbit lovers, in addition to how to sign up to the news update email service.

OTHER STUFF

• Catch up on all the latest news from the ubiquitous producer on the News pages.

• Get the complete lowdown on the 'low-profile studio recluse' on the About pages, and if you must know more, you will find a complete list of links to articles and reviews written about him over the years, and a year-by-year chronology on the History channel.

• Leave your proclamation of devotion, and read others' messages on the Guestbook pages.

• Search the entire site by date and reference term on, well, the Search page.

• The Links page contains fairly extensive links to ecommerce, related artists, and fan destinations.

A painstakingly produced interactive and simple audio/visual site with everything an Orbit fan could wish to know, plus a little bit extra.

OTHER SITES OF INTEREST

At first glance, the following list may seem to contain some strange bedfellows, but there is a kind of logic to the choices included. The first group included are pretty much the Fathers of Rock; those who have played a defining part in the history of modern rock music. They may not be the latest bright young things, but the ones who are still alive can fill an arena, have a fan base which spans generations, and, as Santana has recently proven, have the occasional worldwide hit.

The next group included are what we think of as Megastars – not quite as long in the tooth as the Fathers, but consistently the best-selling artists in their genre over the past few years, and have a strong media presence, or a loyal cult following.

The third group have been included for fashion's sake. They may be here today, gone tomorrow, but until then we can't tell.

So, with apologies for any omissions, here is our alphabetical list of artists' sites.

A1
Official: **www.a1-online.com**
Fan: **www.a1-home.com**

Abba
Official: **www.abbasite.com**
Fan: **www.abbafiles.com**

Bryan Adams
Official: **www.bryanadams.com**
Fan: **www.badzone.de/index.shtml**

Aerosmith
Official: **www.aerosmith.com**
Fan: **www.aeroforceone.com**

Christina Aguilera
Official: **www.christina-a.com**
or **www.peeps.com/christina**
Fan: **www.christinasgenie.cjb.net**

All Saints
Official: **www.allsaints.uk.com**
Fan: **www.allsaints.ukmix.net**

Aphex Twin
Official: **www.aphex-twin.com**
Fan: **www.aphextwin.org**

music

Richard Ashcroft
Official: **www.richardashcroft.co.uk**
Fan: **http://hem.fyristorg.com/endymion/ashcroft**

Atomic Kitten
Official: **www.atomickitten.co.uk**
Fan: **www.kittencity.co.uk**

The B52s
Official: **www.theb52s.com**
Fan: **www.b52s.net**

Backstreet Boys
Official: **www.backstreetboys.com**
Fan: **www.backstreet.net**

Barenaked Ladies
Official: **www.barenakedladies.com**
Fan: **www.bnl.org**

Beastie Boys
Official: **www.beastieboys.com/**
or **www.grandroyal.com**
Fan: **www.beastieboogloo.digitalspace.net**

The Beatles
Official: **www.lookon.net**
Fan: **www.beatlelinks.net**
or **www.legacylinks.com** for a useful portal
for 60's rock n' roll information.

Paul McCartney
Official: **www.mplcommunications.com**
Fan: **www.macca-l.ne**

The Beautiful South
Official: **www.beautifulsouth.co.uk**
Fan: **www.liarsbar.btinternet.co.uk**

The Bee Gees
Official: **www.beegees.net**
Fan: **www.beegeesfanclub.org**

Beenie Man
no specific fan site – a good genre site is:
www.dancehallreggae.com

Mary J Blige
Official: **www.mjblige.com**
Fan: **www.geocities.com/thebwproject**

Bjork, see p.165

Blink 182
Official: **www.blink182.com**
Fan: **www.blink-one-eighty-two.com**

Blondie
Official: **www.blondie.net**
Fan: **www.blondie.ausbone.net**

The Bloodhound Gang
Official: **www.bloodhoundgang.com**

Boards of Canada
Official: **www.boardsofcanada.com**

Bomfunk MCs
No specific site – find info on:
www.sonymusiceurope.com

Bon Jovi
Official: **www.bonjovi.com**
Fan: **www.backstagejbj.com**

Bomb the Bass, see p.171.

David Bowie
Official: **www.davidbowie.com**
Fan: **www.teenagewildlife.com**

Boyzone
Official: **www.boyzone.co.uk**
Fan: www.**boyzonesite.cjb.net**

Ronan Keating
www.ronankeating.net

Stephen Gately
www.stephengately.com

Mikey Graham
www.mikeygraham.co.uk

Billy Bragg
Official: **www.billybragg.co.uk**

Fan: **www.lilypad.demon.co.uk/bragg/**

Toni Braxton
Official: **www.tonibraxtononline.com**
Fan: **www.musicfanclubs.org/tonibraxton**

Cabaret Voltaire, see p.171

Mariah Carey
Official: **www.mcarey.com**
Fan: **www.mariahcarey.org**

Catatonia
Official: **www.catatonia.net/**
Fan: **www.easyweb.easynet.co.uk**

Nick Cave
Official: **www.mutelibtech.com/mute/**
Fan: **www.nick-cave.com**

Chemical Brothers
Official: **www.the-raft.com/chemicalbros/**
Fan: **www.musicfanclubs.org/chemical**

Chumbawumba
Official: **www.chumba.com**
Fan: **www.koeln-bonn.net/chumba**

Eric Clapton
Official: **www.repriserec.com/ericclapton**
Fan: **www.eric-clapton.co.uk**

music

The Clash
Fan: **www.geocites.com/internetclash**
/index.html

Leonard Cohen
Fan: **www.netsonic.fi/~ja/cohen**

Coldcut
Official: **www.ninjatune.net/coldcut**
Radio: **www.solidsteel.com**

Phil Collins
Official: (label) **www.atlantic-records.com**
Fan: **www.philcollinscage.com**

Common
Official: **www.com-mon.com**
Fan: **www.okayplayer.com**

The Corrs
Official: **www.corrs.net**
Fan: **www.corrsonline.com**

Elvis Costello
Official: **www.wbr.com/elvis**
Fan: **www.costello.online.com**

Cypress Hill
Official: **www.cypressonline.com**
or **www.soulassassins.com**
Fan: **www.cypressconnection.com**

Daft Punk
Official: **www.daftpunk.com (label) the-raft**
.com/daftpunk.html

D'Angelo
Official: **www.okayplayer.com/dangelo/**
Fan: **www.dangelolive.com**

Daphne & Celeste
Official: **www.daphneandceleste.com**

Craig David
Official: **www.craigdavid.co.uk**
Fan: www.**craigdavid.cjb.net/**

Death In Vegas
Official: **www.death-in-vegas.co.uk**
and **www.dspace.dial.pipex.com/planet**
anderson

Alice Deejay
Official: **www.alice-deejay.net**

The Deftones
Official: **www.deftones.com**
Fan: **www.home.dencity.com/thebhg**

De La Soul
Official: **www.multsanta.madvision**
.co.uk/dela
Label: **www.tommyboy.com**

Fan: **www.delasoul.org/spitkickercom/**

Derrick May
www.submerge.com/APPages/DerrickMay.html

Destiny's Child
Official: **www.destinyschild.com/**
Fan: **www.dc-unplugged.com/**

Digital Noise Allstars
Official: **www.digitalnoiseallstars.co.uk**

Dilated Peoples
Official: **www.dilatedpeoples.com**
Fan: **www.bounce.to/jurassic5**

Celine Dion
Official: **www.celineonline.com**
Fan: **www.celine-dion.org**

The Doors
Official: **www.thedoors.com**
Fan: **www.thedoors.ch**

Dr Dre
Official: **www.dre2001.com**
Fan: **www.dr-dre.com www.dreday.com**

Dubstar
Official: **www.food-records.co.uk**
Fan: **easyweb.easynet.co.uk/~neilh**

Duran Duran
Official: **www.duranduran.com**
Fan: **www.plasticgirl.co.uk**

Bob Dylan
Official: **www.bobdylan.com**
Fan: **www.expectingrain.com**

Elastica
Official: **www.elasticaband.com**
Fan: **www.elasticated.com**

Missy Elliot
Official: **www.missy-elliott.com**
or **www.shesabitch.com/**

music

Fan: **wwwclubs.yahoo.com/clubs/ darealmissyelliottworld**

Eminem
Official: **www.eminem.com**
Fan: **www.slimshadyworld.co.uk**

Brian Eno
Official: **www.brianeno.com**
Fan: **music.hyperreal.org/artists/brian_eno**
Radio: **www.dv103.com/**

Gloria Estefan
Official: **www.gloriafan.com**
Fan: **www.almetco.com/estefan/gloria-1.html**

Eurythmics
Official: **www.eurythmics.net**
Fan: **www.vibber.dk/eurythmistan**

Everything But The Girl
www.ebtg.com

Fatboy Slim
Official: **www.astralwerks.com**
or **www.skint.net or www.normancook.net**
Fan: **www.fatboyslim.org.uk**

Bryan Ferry and Roxy Music
Official: **http://bryanferrydirect.com/**
Fan: **http://www.dlc.fi/~hope/index.html**

Finley Quaye
Official: **www.finleyquaye.com**

Flaming Lips
Official: **www.flaminglips.com/**
Main: **www.geocities.com/~notyep1/flips/ flips.htm**

Fleetwood Mac
Official: **www.repriserec.com/fleetwoodmac**
Fan: **www.fleetwoodmac.net**

Fugees
Official: **www.fugees.net**

Lauryn Hill
Fans: **www.lauryn-hill .com**

Wyclef Jean
Fans:: **www.wyclef.com**

The Future Sound of London
Official: **www.the-raft.com/fsol**

Gangstarr
Fan:**www.gangstarr.8m.com**

Garbage
Official: **www.garbage.com**
Fan: **www.geocities.com/SouthBeach/ Boardwalk/2249/garbage.html**

Laurent Garnier
www.laurentgarnier.com

Marvin Gaye
Official: **www.motown.com/classicmotown/f**
Fan: **www.sedgsoftware.com/marvin/**

Genesis
Official: **www.genesis-web.co.uk**

Gomez
Official: **www.gomez.co.uk**
or **www.liquidskin.co.uk**
Fan: **www.jbingham.freeserve.co.uk**

Macy Gray
official: **www.macygray.com**
Fan: **www.geocities.com/macygrayoo**

Grateful Dead
Official: **www.dead.net**
fan: **www.gdlive.com**

Gravediggaz
Official: **www.peeps.com/gravediggaz**

Grooverider
www.grooverider.com/

Guns n' Roses
Official: **www.gunsnrosesdirect.com**
Fan: **www.lostrose.com**

A Guy Called Gerald
Official: **www.studio-k7.com**
Fan:**www.homepages.force9.net/king1**

Hanson
Official: **www.hansononline.com**
Fan: **www.stas.net/sami/**

Ben Harper
Official: **www.virginrecords.com/ben_harper**
Fan: **http://www.web.one.net.au/~watsun/main.htm**

music

PJ Harvey
Official: **www.pjh.org**
Fan: **www.geocities.com/Harveyfizz/index.html**

Heather Nova
Official: **(fanclub)www.heathernova.org**
or **www.heathernova.co.uk**
Fan: **www.valmccown.com/heather/index_bottom.shtml**

Jimi Hendrix
Official: **www.mcarecords.com/artists**
Fan: **/jhendrix.virtualave.net**

Hieroglyphics
Label **www.Hieroglyphics.com**

Billie Holiday
Official: **www.cmgww.com/music/holiday**
Fan: **http://www.users.bart.nl/~ecduzit/billie.htm**

Whitney Houston
Official: **www.aristarec.com/aristaweb/WhitneyHouston/index.html**
Fan: **www.whitney-fan.com**
or **www.simplywhitney.co.uk**

Ice Cube
Official: **www.icecube.com**
Fan: **www.icecube.cjb.net**

Iron Maiden
Official: **www.ironmaiden.co.uk**
Fan: **www.ironmaiden.webvis.net**

Jackson Five
Fan: **www.geocities.com/SoHo/Studios/7329/JACKSONS.HTML**
or **http://members.aol.com/mikeljaxn/jacksons/jfive.htm**

Michael Jackson
Official: **www.mjnet.com**
Fan: **www.mjifc.com**
or **www.geneva-link.ch/khanmail**

Janet Jackson
Official: **www.missjanet.com**
Fan: **www.janet.nu**

Jamiroquai
Official: **www.jamiroquai.co.uk**
Fan: **www.jamiroquai.com**

Jane's Addiction
Official: **www.wbr.com/janesaddiction/**
Fan: **www.one-percent.com**

Elton John
Aids Foundation: **www.ejaf.org**

MCA Records: **http://www.mcarecords.com**
Fan: **www.eltonfan.com**

Joy Division
Fan: **www.warren.org.uk/music/joyd**

Jungle Brothers
Official: **www.junglebrothers.com**
Fan: **www.home.ici.net/~tessier/ibeez.htm**

Jurassic Five
Official: **www.jurassic5.com**

Kelis
Official: **www.kelis.com/**
Fan: **www.kelis.sexypage.net**

BB King
Official: **www.bbking.com**
Fan: **www.geocites.com/BourbonStreet/1242**

Carole King
Fan: **http://members.home.net/caroleking**

Kraftwerk
www.kraftwerk.com

Led Zepplin
Official: **www.led-zeppelin.com/**

Leftfield
Official: **www.leftfield-online.com/**

Fan: **www.djdust.demon.co.uk/leftfield**

Lil' Kim
Official: **www.lilkim.com**
Fan: **www.lilkimwebsite.simplenet.com**

LimpBizkit
Official: **www.limp-bizkit.com**

LL Cool J
Official: **www.llcoolj.com**
Fan: **www.angelfire.com/pop/llcoolj/**

Lonestar
www.lonestar-band.com/

Courtney Love
Official: **www.holemusic.com**
Fan: **www. sweetcherrie.com**

Lucy Pearl
Official: **www.lucypearl.com**
Fan: **www.members.xoom.com/_XMCM
/lucypearl**

Madonna, see p.179

Manic Street Preachers
Official: **www.manics.co.uk/**
Fan: **www.lukemanic.com**

music

Aimee Mann
Official: **www.aimeemann.com**
Fan: **www.dayfree.robotstories.com**

Marillion
Official: **www.marillion.com**
Fan: **www.multimania.com/edwood/**

Dean Martin
Official: **http://www.deanmartinfan center.com**
Fan: **http://members.xoom.com/deansplace 1/index.htm**

Massive Attack
Official: **www.massiveattack.com**
or **www.melankolic.astralwerks.com /massive**

Meat Beat Manifesto, see p.171

Metallica
Official: **www.metallica.com**
Fan: **www.encycmet.com/**

George Michael
Official: **www.aegean.net**
Fan: **www.yogworld.com**

Kylie Minogue
Official: **www.kylie.com**
Fan: **www.kylie.co.uk**

Joni Mitchell
Official: **www.JoniMitchell.com**
Fan: **http://imusic.com/showcase/ contemporary/jonimitchell.html**

Moby
Official: **www.mutelibtech.com/mute/moby**
Fan: **www.moby.org**

Alanis Morrissette
Official: **www.repriserec.com/alanis/**
Fan: **www.alanismorrissette.net**

Morrissey
Fan: **www.morrissey-solo.com/**

Mos Def
Official: **www.rawkus.com/mosdef.htm**

Fan: **www.mason.gmu.edu/~dtursan.rammy**

Mouse On Mars
www.mouseonmars.com

Muse
Official:**www.muse-official.com**
Fan: **www.muse.org.uk**

Nas
Official: **www.iamnas.com**
Fan: **www.homestead.com/pg2000_99/NasIsLike.html**

New Order
Fan:**slashmc.rice.edu/ceremony/ceremony.html**

Nine Inch Nails
www.9inchnails.com

Nirvana
Official: **www.geffen.com**
Fan:**www.nirvanapage.com**

Oasis
Official: **www.oasisinet.com**
Fan: **www.oasisnews.com**

Sinead O'Connor
Official: **www.atlantic-records.com**

Fan: **www.geocities.com/SunsetStrip/Backstage/9922**

The Orb
Fan: **www.theorb.com**

Orbital
Official: **www.loopz.co.uk**

Pearl Jam
Official: **www.tenclub.net**
or **www.sonymusic.com/artists/pearljam**
Fan: **www.evenflow.org**

A Perfect Circle
Official: **aperfectcircle.com**
Fan: **aperfectcircle.org/**

The Pharcyde
Official: **www.thepharcyde.com**
Fan: **www.geocities.com/southbeach/cove/8145**

Pink
Official: **www.pinkspage.com**

Pink Floyd
Fan:**www.pinkfloyd-co.com**

Gram Parsons
Official: **www.gramparsons.com**
Fan: **www.nashville.net/~kate/gram.html**

music

Billie Piper
Official: **www.c3.vmg.co.uk/billie**
Fan: **www.billie-piper.com**

Pixies
Official: **www.4ad.com/artists/pixies/death tothepixies/index.html**
fan: **www.ozemail.com.au/~thrashin/pixies** or **www.pixies.com.co**

Placebo
Official: **www.thebsh.com** or **www.the-raft.com/placebo**
Fan: **www.glamkitty.tripod.com/placebo**

Plastikman and Richie Hawtin
Fan:**www.m-nus.com**

Portishead
Official: **www.portishead.co.uk**
Fan: **www.portishead.4mg.com**

Prince, see p.182

Elvis Presley
Official: **www.elvis-presley.com**
Fan: **www.elvis.com.au**

The Prodigy
Official: **www.xl-recordings.com.**
Fan: **www.theprodigy.org**

Queen
Official: **www.queenonline.com**

Radiohead, see p.173

Rage Against the Machine
www.ratm.com

The Ramones
Official: **www.officialramones.com**
Fan: **www.venus.spaceports.com/~ivo/ ramones.html**

Red Hot Chilli Peppers
Official: **www.redhotchilipeppers.net**
Fan: **www.rpi.net.au/~mutha**

Reef
Official: **www.reef.co.uk**

Lou Reed
Official: **www.loureed.org**
Fan: **www.members.aol.com/olandem4 /reed.html**

R.E.M
Official: **www.emhq.com**
Fan: **www.rem-fan.com**

Cliff Richard
Official: **www.cliffrichard.org**
Fan: **www.sircliffrichard.dk**

Rolling Stones
Official: **www.stones.com**
or **www.the-rolling-stones.com**
Fan: **www.stones.net**

Diana Ross
Official: **www.dianaross.co.uk**
Fan:**www.thedivadigest.com**

Run DMC
Official: **www.arista.com/aristaweb/Run DMC/artist_index.html**
Fan: **www.thadweb.com/rundmc**

S Club 7
Official: **www.sclub.com/**
Fan: **www.sclub7online.net/**

Sade
Official: **www.epicenter.com (label)**
Fan: **www.auraland.com/sade**

Carlos Santana
Official: **www.santana.com**

Sasha
Official: **www.djsasha.net**

Savage Garden
Official: **www.savagefan.com**

Sex Pistols
Fan: **www.geocities.com/SunsetStrip/ Balcony/5910/**
or: **www.come.to/lovekills**

Simon & Garfunkel
Official: **www.sonymusic.com/artists/ SimonAndGarfunkel/index.html**
Fan: www.**songfta.cjb.net**

DJ Shadow
Official: **www.dj-shadow.8m.com**

Tupac Shakur
Official: **www.tupacshakur.com**
Fan: **http://www.tupac.net**

Simply Red
Official: **www.simplyred.co.uk**
Fan: **www.zen.co.uk/redweb**

Frank Sinatra
Fan: **http://www.sinatraclub**

Sisqo
Official: **www.sisqo.com/**

Slipknot
Official: **www.slipknot2.com**
Fan: **www.crowz.org**

music

Smashing Pumpkins
Official: www.smashingpumpkins.com
Fan: www.smashing-pumpkins.net

The Smiths
Fan:www.people.we.mediaone.net/subgenius/index.html

Johnny Marr
Official: www.jmarr.com

Sonique
Official: www.soniqueonline.com

Britney Spears
Official: www.britneyspears.com/www.britney.com
Fan: www.britneyspearsfan.com

Spice Girls
Official: www.C3.vmg.co.uk

Emma
Fan : http://www.emmabunton.com.tj

Geri
Official: http://www.geri-halliwell.com//http://www.emichrysalis.co.uk/
Fan : http://www.mbuzz.com/geri/

Mel B
Official: www.melanie-b.com/

Mel C
Official: http://www.northern-star.co.uk
Fan:http://www.tornado.pair.com/melaniec/

Victoria
Official:www.members.tripod.co.uk/~victoriaspalace.com
or http://www.geocities.com/SunsetStrip/Backstage/8975/

Spiller
Official: www.positivarecords.co.uk

Bruce Springsteen
Official: www.brucespringsteen.net
Fan: home.theboots.net/theboots/home.html

Squarepusher
Official: www.warprecords.com/squarepusher
Fan: www.squarepusher.com

808 State
Official: www.808state.com
Fan: www.members.tripod.com/~mad808/

Steps
Official: www.stepsofficial.com
Fan: www.gensteps.co.uk

Sterephonics
Official: **www.stereophonics.com**

Rod Stewart
Official: **www.rodstewartlive.com**

Sting
Official: **www.stingchronicity.co.uk**
 or **sting.compaq.com**

The Stone Roses
Fan: www.youaremyworld.co.uk
 or **www.stoneroses.fsnet.co.uk**
Ian Brown: **www.ianbrown.co.uk**

Super Furry Animals
Official: **www.superfurry.com**
Fan: **www.playitcool.co.uk**

TLC
Official: **www.tlcfanmail.com**
Fan: **www.tlcgalaxy.com**

Toploader
Official: **www.toploader.go.to**
Fan: **www.toploader.go.to**

Travis
Official: **www.travisonline.com**
Fan: **wwwmembers.tripod.com/~yeoyl /travismenu.html**

T-Rex & Marc Bolan
Fan: **www.easyweb.co.uk/~rthomas/rexdal /mystic.html**

Tribe Called Quest
Official: **www.atcq.com**
Fan: **www.slumvillage.net/**

Tricky
Official: **www.trickyonline.com/**
Fan: **www.hauntedink.com/tricky**

Truesteppers
Official: **www.nuliferecords.com**

Tina Turner
Offiicial: **www.tina-turner.com**
ecommerce: **www.tinaturnerdirect.com**
Fan: **www.sidlovestina.com**

Shania Twain
Official: **www.shania-twain.com**
Fan: **www.shania.com**

Two Lone Swordsmen
Fan: **www.music.hyperreal.org/flightpath**

U2
Official: **http://www.u2.com**
Fan: **http://www.interface.com**

music

Underground Resistance
www.undergroundresistance.com

Underworld
Official: **www.dirty.org**
Fan: **www.senses.co.uk**

Van Morrison
Official: **http://www.harmone.com/bands/index.html**

Suzanne Vega
Official: **http://www.vega.net**
Fan: **www.groovybass.com/suzanne.vega**

Vengaboys
Official: **www.vengaboys.com**
Fan: **www.people.a2000.nl/tax/vengaboys.html#**

The Verve
Official: **www.the-raft.com/theverve/**
Fan: **www.odc.net/~ssharma/verve**
or **www.angelfire.com/biz3/theverve/**

Paul Weller
Official: **www.paul-weller.com**
Fan: **www.columbia.edu/%7Eals3**

Westlife
Official: **www.westlife.co.uk**
Fan: **come.to/westlife**

Barry White
Official: **www.barrywhitemusic.com/**
Fan: **www.pklein.demon.nl/bw.htm**

Robbie Williams
Official: **www.robbiewilliams.com/**

Wu Tang Clan
Fan: **www.wunation.com**

Neil Young
Official: **www.neilyoung.com**
Fan: **http://HyperRust.org**

Frank Zappa
Official: **http://www.zappa.com**
Fan: **www.hearbloodymusic.com/frankzappa**

online broadcasting

This chapter contains the far-flung stations that defy classification. Like the very best artists, the sites reviewed here are too ridiculous, abstract or just too sublime to pin down to any tired old genre. Each of these sites takes an aspect of music-related culture and moulds it into a bizarre, intellectual, trashy or slippery send-up. Welcome to the corner inhabited by the lone rangers, the funked-up cybergoths and other long-forgotten sonic surfers. These are the interesting people with a penchant for the unpredictable. Tool up, get set and prepare to warp.

music

overall rating:
★ ★ ★ ★ ★

classification:
sound games fun

updated:
irregular

navigation:
★ ★ ★ ★ ★

content:
★ ★ ★ ★

readability:
★ ★ ★ ★ ★

speed:
★ ★ ★ ★ ★

US

http://www.audiogames.com
Audiogames

Audiogames' raison d'être is 12 ways to waste time playing with music. This site is in a class of its own, dedicated to devising wicked little ways for the sonic surfer to turn their PC into a Utopian smorgasbord of sound, and offering video games for kids obsessed with music. Set in a bright yellow, no-frills, professional and easy-to-navigate environment, each game is listed with a brief summary of what to expect, what you'll need to play and a simple hyperlink to progress to the starting line. Wasting time is rarely so much fun, so come and blur the line between musical composition and playful recreation.

COOL STUFF

• All the games are pretty damn fine, but we especially enjoyed the online turntablist mission turntables.de. – putting the Flash into Grandmaster, apparently. And all the games are either generative, stochastic, interactive, or all three. Whatever that means, it sounds cool.

• The FAQ gives you the full lowdown on the facts behind this recreational piece of genius, just so you know.

• Leave that well-worn email address in the mailing section and be the first to know when there's more sound ways to have fun.

Sound ways to waste time for the blissed-out sonic-surf generation. Or something.

http://www.putsch.co.uk
Putsch

Software: Flash and Macromedia.

This site – the future in non-linear media, no less – is so out of the league that it should have its own chapter. Put together by the cream of the UK's interactive design talent and multimedia artists, Putsch is the mother site to a host of funked-up, bizarre, hilarious, and fantastic babies. Visit www.h69.net for a series of animations that will make you wonder why the web isn't this good elsewhere. Fully sound and Flash-enabled, each disc link on the h69 motherboard will take you to another window and another sexy sonic cyberspace planet, be it the balloon blowjob game or the funky, high-rise, Red Riding Hood tale.

The superbly designed Konspiracy.co.uk has amusing and inspiring interviews with some of the best new media talent around, such as Brighton's kerb (the talent behind past EMI web projects, and now the driving force behind live music event company Mean Fiddler's fledgling webcasting site Meanfiddler.com, where you can catch exclusive coverage of Reading and V2000). You can catch some cool digital animation and stream sounds in the gallery section of ecommerce agency link www.vir2l.com, while www.linkedup.com is a well-informed resource for searching the best use of design and technology on the web, although it can be a bit slow on slower modem connections. Don't bother with ziggen.com – it's a dead link.

overall rating:
★ ★ ★ ★ ★
classification:
music & animation
updated:
weekly
navigation:
★ ★ ★ ★ ★
content:
★ ★ ★ ★
readability:
★ ★ ★ ★ ★
speed:
★ ★ ★ ★ ★
UK

COOL STUFF

• Metemphsychosis is the fine station for a 'loose collective' of experimental musicians and artists, where you can catch the latest news, views and MP3s. By the way, metempsychosis, means passing of the soul at death into another body, or transmigration. Nice.

• H69.net is the ultimate interactive, sound animation playground area of award-winning web design agency Flammable Jam, the creators of the excellent streaming site for Scottish radio station Beat106 (www.beat106.com) and festival organisers Homelands (www.homelands.co.uk). It's hard to highlight one cool feature here, as it's all pretty cool. The site basically consists of a series of music animations; we recommend Birdwatching, the video game guide, blowjob, birdy, scream, and Little Red Riding Hood.

• Linkdup.com is a treasure trove of reviews and links to some of the most cutting-edge sites, including the supa animation site www.destroyrockcity.com and www.motown.com. All sites are catalogued and cross-referenced for simple search pleasure.

• Submit your own musical masterpieces for consideration for the Surfstation CD and read about the art talent behind many of the sites mentioned here via the Surfstation link.

• Click to Konspiracy to sample delights of real musical artists in the music section of the Features channel, and get in touch to submit your own efforts. There is a nice and well-populated Java chatroom, and you can browse the board designs (skate) and submit your own works of art in the Show us Your Board section.

• Get some best-of-breed wallpaper and screensavers in the gallery section, vir2l. Along with the funky interactive and motion sections, and the choice of three sublime soundtracks, this site isn't unjustified in claiming to be an introduction to the next generation.

• Designiskinky.net profiles and links a raft of the cream-of-web design talent on the web. See what both the sonic and aesthete surf should really be about.

• Urbanexpress is an animated and stills site dedicated to 'exploring urban mundanity – a travel guide to the forgotten places we see every day'. Superb.

A jewel in the crown of sonic cyberspace creations.

music

overall rating:
★ ★ ★ ★ ★

classification:
music art culture musings

updated:
irregular

navigation:
★ ★ ★ ★ ★

content:
★ ★ ★ ★

readability:
★ ★ ★ ★ ★

speed:
★ ★ ★ ★ ★

US

http://www.urbansounds.com
Urban Sounds

Software: Flash.

Urban Sounds is one of the most aesthetically pleasing, pure-of-motive, intellectual and plain inspired sites around, run by a San Francisco-based group who describe themselves as an 'amorphous collective of writers, Web developers, artists, designers, composers, musicians and DJs who have a desire to extend their common interest in dance and electronic music both above and below ground'. Couldn't have put it better myself. The site is clean, easy to navigate and contains sounds, interviews and essays on the unsung musical heroes of our time. You simply won't find most of this stuff anywhere else, unfettered by cheap moneymaking attempts; there is no sales pitch, either from within the site or from outside advertisers. Sublime.

COOL STUFF

• Read articles in the Thumbnail Music channel containing sounds and interviews from some of the greatest living composers and pre-eminent song-writers, producers, DJs and artists of our time. Stimulating, intellectual and of a high quality.

• The reviews section has intelligent, witty and irreverent viewpoints on all the latest electronic music releases (think Richie Hawtin). In their words, 'not simple floor bangers'.

• Each month, a DJ is invited to post mixes and reveal his all-time top ten.

• The links section is one of the most exhaustive lists of hard-to-find independent experimental electronic artists and their labels; think Two Lone Swordsmen or Underground Resistance.

Urban Sounds aims to be a serious and visually engaging forum for the discussion and exploration of electronic music and its many genres. We think that largely it succeeds.

music

overall rating:
★ ★ ★ ★
classification:
sex & gossip
updated:
irregular
navigation:
★ ★ ★ ★
content:
★ ★ ★ ★
readability:
★ ★ ★ ★
speed:
★ ★ ★ ★
US

http://www.groupiecentral.com
Groupie Central

This site is an unashamed, non-commercial community of star-struck young lovers swapping tales of their rock'n'rolling. Think trailer park. Think Courtney love or L7. Those babes have nothing on these girls. Obviously a homepage effort, these clunky chintz wallpapered pages shout their pop gossip loud and proud in gigantic coloured text. Forget trying to sneak a peak on your grandmother's PC. This site is built for the loud, out and proud, or in their own words: 'followers of music who are young, female and gorgeous.' We'll take their word for it. This site is the cream of the unapologetic pop-trash-gossip culture and we love it.

COOL STUFF

• The FAQ section is a must if you're on the outside looking in, as most of us are. The FAQ answers your questions and declares the honour of the groupie in no uncertain terms. It is adamant about the difference between a groupie and an obsessed fan (groupies are in touch with reality), about why stereotypes should be abandoned, and declares that they're not all star fuckers [sic] ('some groupies are looking for love and romance, while others only want a friendship'). Also find out why it's apparently not demeaning to be a groupie, and how you could join them. Girlfriend, this is illuminating stuff.

• The Message Board is open to anyone wanting to share their starstruck tales. Only for the very brave.

• The News & Gossip pages are where you'll get all the latest hair-raising stories about the sordid lives of famous lovers. The best section is the blind item bonanza, where outrageous claims are made, leaving you guessing which famous dadrock star it could be. The gossip pages are, of course, what the site is all about. Made up of tittle-tattle shockers and the plain obvious, these are mostly drawn from emails sent to the site, the message board and celebrity books and documentaries.

OTHER STUFF

• The Groupies, Wives and Lovers section has the lowdown on any famous girlies you can think of who've been romantically linked with a rock star, with biogs on everyone from Mariah Carey and Angie Bowie to Yasmin Le Bon. A place to stoke up your jealousy, if you're that way inclined.

• The Album Covers, Music Videos, and Articles & Interviews pages are painstaking archives of the media appearances of famous 'significant others'.

The out-and-proud world of sex and celebrity. Pure trailer trash pop gossip, this site is the ultimate nod to the jaded post-modern aesthetic. We love it.

music

overall rating:	★ ★ ★ ★
classification:	clothing ecommerce
updated:	weekly
navigation:	★ ★ ★ ★
content:	★ ★ ★ ★
readability:	★ ★ ★ ★
speed:	★ ★ ★ ★
US	

http://www.yumpop.com
Yum Pop

Yum Pop is part of a family of San Francisco-based funky threads sites. Designed with a pure bubblegum pop aesthetic, the t-shirts, accessories and posters are the last word in pop girl style. Yum Pop, Oopsy-Daisy, Emily and Eleven-Eleven are essentially a virtual shop, but it's the kind of shop you want to hang out in and meet your mates at. This is what the web is all about: getting down with cool San Francisco threads and wowing the jealous lovelies at parties when you say your threads aren't from Top Shop. Worth a look.

COOL STUFF

• Tees is where you can browse the gorgeous t-shirts.

• The Accessories channel is where you can find cute purses, key rings and badges.

• Cute 'n' sew is the place to head for hoodies.

• Freebies is the place for posters, desktop art and screensavers.

• Catch the bargains from Yum Pop and Cosmic Debris by getting on the email mailing list, linked at the top right of the page.

Bubblegum pop clothing from San Francisco. Look the part.

OTHER SITES OF INTEREST

Cool Homepages
www.coolhomepages.com
This site is a fantastic portal resource for daily updated site reviews and links worth taking a peak at. All sites are categorised by a wide range of subsections, including portals, ezines and audio/sound.

Nosedive
http://www.nosedive.com
Sound and graphics of the highest order, this site is a ten minute web animation set to experimental sounds. Type in the URL, sit back and prepare to be amazed.

le piano graphique
http://www.pianographique.com
Select from a variety of musical styles and proceed to the composition area to lay down your latest sound-and-vision masterpiece. Whilst you build up your track from the pre-recorded loops and stabs, the visuals do the same, developing a themed album cover to accompany your sounds.

The SampleHead Web Community
http://www.samplehead.com
The SampleHead Web Community was created by Phat Drum Loops creator, Mhat Bernstein, to serve as a gateway to a small

circle of independent websites that offer the best resources and information on beat-collecting, crate-digging, production, and related downloadables. Apparently, member sites are hand-picked and included for their merits, not for the size of the owner's wallet.

stop press...

The internet moves fast. Here are two five-star sites which came online just as we were about to go to press and which just couldn't be left out...

www.popworld

Popworld

Software: Flash, Realplayer.

The very recently launched Popworld is the brainchild of ex-Spice Girls manager and current S Club 7 minder Simon Fuller. The man with the Midas touch looks well placed to succeed again with this site. The site is fully interactive, complete with voice-overs from the stars. It's also neon-bright and fun to play with: the ultimate virtual playground for Britney and Westlife wannabes. If you're any kind of switched-on kid, you're probably already collecting the Pop Points: a neat way for kids to buy on the web. From early 2001 Cadbury products will carry Pop Points which young music fans can spend in the Popworld shop. Full marks.

overall rating:
★ ★ ★ ★ ★

classification:
bubblegum pop homepage

updated:
daily

navigation:
★ ★ ★ ★

content:
★ ★ ★ ★ ★

readability:
★ ★ ★ ★

speed:
★ ★ ★ ★ ★

UK

COOL STUFF

• The Popworld shop sells a variety of singles, albums, and Popworld T-shirts and accessories.

• Channel two is Popworld TV - 24/7 streaming sugar-pop hits, webcasting of the day in the life of a popstar and cool pix.

• View the latest Pepsi Chart and listen to sample clips of the entire top 40, the Popworld Chart and the best pop dancers chart (as voted by Popworlders) in Channel Six.

• Poppost allows you to send messages to your pals within the Popworld site in real time.

• Channel Eight is where girls really want to hang out and get beauty tips from the likes of Billie and Girlthing.

• Channel nine has some really cool games such as a version of that old favourite Space Invaders, only this time it's the stage that's being invaded. Also some very hot tickets to be won - such as tickets for your whole class to see Westlife - in Click2win.

OTHER STUFF

• Popworld Today in channel one is a rolling news service. It serves up the kind of pop news little girls will love, such as Girlthing's sleeping habits and Britney Spears' childhood prankster confessions.

• Check your horoscope, gossip and pop diary in the Fox-e channel at number four (with Capital's DJ Fox).

• The My Popword channel three is all about voting, swapping and getting cool stuff. You can also send in a picture of yourself for display.

www.toryumon.co.uk
Toryumon

Software: Flash, Realplayer.

Toryumon is a brand-new dance music site which aims to showcase new talent, providing a pretty funky space for new music to be sampled, downloaded and voted on as part of the Toryumon battle. Sony says it created Toryumon to help anyone who wishes to participate in the ever-expanding dance music culture, whether an established producer with tracks you want the world to hear, an enthusiast looking for innovative music, a record label on the hunt for fresh talent, or simply a curious observer. The site has gone some way to getting attention of serious established dance industry heads to provide context, advice and judging on the site. Howie B (musician, producer, DJ and label owner) has apparently committed himself to the project, and is involved in everything from judging tracks to chairing a forum on production techniques and new equipment. Although this site looks good and each section is an easylink from the homepage, a certain amount of guesswork is needed to find simple information, such as the voting and uploading procedure. In short, this site is in desperate need of a catchall FAQ section. There is no information about the contractual arrangements an artist undertakes when submitting their music to the site, which is a bit offputting.

overall rating:
★ ★ ★ ★
classification:
unsigned dance music
updated:
irregularly
navigation:
★ ★ ★ ★
content:
★ ★ ★ ★ ★
readability:
★ ★ ★ ★
speed:
★ ★ ★ ★ ★
UK

COOL STUFF

• The News section serves up a tasty selection of news from across the UK club and dance scene and has interviews and reviews with cream talent such as the likes of ex-Galliano members new projects and Basement Jaxx - complete with links to the relevant artist/club/organisation's websites.

• The plug-in page has links to download the new Sony minidisc quality and compatible ryu-ring player software - complete with exhaustive and easy-to-follow instructions.

• The Battleground channel is where you get to vote for the shortlisted dance tracks submitted to the site .

• Take a peak at the full range of dance charts via the charts link in the News channel – such as the cool cuts and underground charts. A specialist chart is also supplied monthly by a DJ or specialist record store – such as London's Blackmarket, plus, or course, Toryumon's own top ten.

• The Tech channel has news and reviews of the latest DJ and mixing hard and software, plus a music production beginners guide and handy advice kit with all you need to elevate yourself from your bedroom and the local pub to super-rich DJ status.

• The knowledge section has a vast number of useful links (complete with reviews) and is divided into technical, songwriting and many other handy sections. A good starting point for the serious sonic surf.

OTHER STUFF

• The artist info pages has details of all the artists from around the world who successfully entered the battleground with uploaded tracks, while you can listen to said masterpieces - sorted by artist name or song title in the Tracks channel.

• Access webcasts and studio interviews in the Events channel.

• Discuss musical styles, swap event news and look for talent for your new 'band' on the message boards - linked via the community channel. Only for the extremely dedicated.

A useful showcase, news and advice resource for dance heads.

glossary of internet terms

Accelerators Add-on programs, which speed up browsing.

Acceptable Use Policy These are the terms and conditions of using the internet. They are usually set by organisations, who wish to regulate an individual's use of the internet. For example, an employer might issue a ruling on the type of email which can be sent from an office.

Access Provider A company which provides access to the internet, usually via a dial-up account. Many companies such as AOL and Dircon charge for this service, although there are an increasing number of free services such as Freeserve, Lineone and Tesco.net. Also known as an Internet Service Provider.

Account A user's internet connection, with an Access/ Internet Service Provider, which usually has to be paid for.

Acrobat Reader Small freely-available program, or web browser plug-in, which lets you view a Portable Document Format (PDF) file.

Across Lite Plug-in which allows you to complete crossword puzzles online.

Address Location name for email or internet site, which is the online equivalent of a postal address. It is usually composed of a unique series of words and punctuation, such as *my.name@house.co.uk*. See also URL.

America Online (AOL) World's most heavily subscribed online service provider.

Animated GIF Low-grade animation technique used on websites.

ASCII Stands for American Standard Code for Information Interchange, It is a coding standard which all computers can recognise, and ensures that if a character is entered on one part of the internet, the same character will be seen elsewhere.

ASCII Art Art made of letters and other symbols. Because it is made up of simple text, it can be recognised by different computers.

ASDL Stands for Asynchronous Digital Subscriber Line, which is a high speed copper wire which will allow rapid transfer of information. Not widely in use at moment, though the government is pushing for its early introduction.

Attachment A file included with an email, which may be composed of text, graphics and sound. Attachments are encoded for transfer across the internet, and can be viewed in their original form by the recipient. An attachment is the equivalent of putting a photograph with a letter in the post.

Bookmark A function of the Netscape Netvigator browser which allows you to save a link to your favourite sites, so that you can return straight there later , without re-entering the address. Favourites in internet Explorer is the same thing.

BPS Abbreviation of Bits Per Second, which is a measure of the speed at which information is transferred or downloaded.

Broadband A type of data transfer medium (usually a cable or wire) which can carry several signals at the same time. Most existing data transfer media are narrowband,and can only carry one signal at a time.

Browse Common term for looking around the web. See also Surfing.

Browser A generic term for the software that allows users to move and look around the Web. Netscape Navigator and Internet Explorer are the ones that most people are familiar with, and they account for 97 percent of web hits.

Bulletin Board Service A BBS is a computer with a telephone connection, which allows you direct contact to upload and download information and converse with other users, via the computer. It was the forerunner to the online services and virtual communities of today.

Cache A temporary storage space on the hard drive of your computer, which stores downloaded websites. When you return to a website, information is retrieved from the cache and displayed much more rapidly. However, this information may not be the most recent version for sites which are frequently updated and you will need to reload the Website address for these.

Chat Talking to other users on the web in real time, but with typed, instead of spoken words. Special software such as ICQ or MIRC is required before you can chat.

Chat Room An internet channel which allows several people to type in their messages, and talk to one another over the internet.

Clickstream The trail left as you 'click' your way around the web.

Codec Any technology which can compress/ decompress data, such as MPEG and MP3.

Content The material on a website that actually relates to the site, and is hopefully of interest or value. Things like adverts are not considered to be part of the content. The term is also used to refer to information on the internet that can be seen by users, as opposed to programming and other background information.

Cookie A cookie is a nugget of information sometimes sent by websites to your hard drive when you visit.They contain such details as what you looked at, what you ordered, and can add more information, so that the website can be customized to suit you.

Cybercafe Cafe where you can use a computer terminal to browse the net for a small fee.

Cyberspace When first coined by the sci-fi author William Gibson, it meant a shared hallucination which occured when people logged on to computer networks. Now, it refers to the virtual space you're in when on the internet.

Dial Up A temporary telephone connection to your ISP's computer and how you make contact with your ISP, each time you log onto the Internet.

Domain The part of an Internet address which identifies an individual computer, and can often be a business or person's name. For example, in the goodwebguide.com the domain name is theGoodWebGuide.

Download Transfer of information from an Internet server to your computer.

Dynamic HTML The most recent version of the HTML standard.

Ecash Electronic cash, used to make transactions on the internet.

Ecommerce The name for business which is carried out over the internet.

Email Mail which is delivered electronically over the internet. Usually comprised of text messages, but can contain illustrations, music and animations. Mail is sent to an email address: the internet equivalent of a postal address.

Encryption A process whereby information is scrambled to produce a 'coded message', so that it can't be read whilst in transit on the internet. The recipient must have decryption software in order to read the message.

Expire Term referring to newsgroup postings which are automatically deleted after a fixed period of time.

Ezine Publication on the web, which is updated regularly.

FAQ Stands for frequently asked questions and is a common section on websites where the most common enquiries and their answers are archived.

Frame A method which splits web pages into several windows.

FTP/File Transfer Protocol Standard method for transporting files across the internet.

GIF/Graphics Interchange Format A format in which graphics are compressed, and a popular method of putting images onto the internet, as they take little time to download.

Gopher The gopher was the precursor of the world wide web and consisted of archives accessed through a menu, usually organised by subject.

GUI/Graphical User Interface. This is the system which turns binary information into the words and images format you can see on your computer screen. For example, instead of seeing the computer language which denotes the presence of your toolbar, you actually see a toolbar.

Hackers A term used to refer to expert programmers who used their skills to break into computer systems, just for the fun of it. Nowadays the word is more commonly associated with computer criminals, or Crackers.

Header Basic indication of what's in an email: who it's from, when it was sent, and what it's about.

Hit When a file is downloaded from a website it is referred to as a 'hit'. Measuring the number of hits is a rough method of counting how many people visit a website. Not wholly accurate as one website can contain many files, so one visit may generate several hits.

Homepage Usually associated with a personal site, but can also refer to the first page on your browser, or the first page of a website.

Host Computer on which a website is stored. A host computer may store several websites, and usually has a fast powerful connection to the internet. Also known as a Server.

HTML/Hypertext Mark-Up Language The computer code used to construct web pages.

HTTP/Hypertext Transfer Protocol The protocol for moving HTML files across the web.

Hyperlink A word or graphic formatted so that when you click on it, you move from one area to another. See also hypertext.

Hypertext Text within a document which is formatted so it acts as a link from one page to another, or from one document to another.

Image Map A graphic which contains hyperlinks.

Interface What you actually see on the computer screen.

Internet One or more computers connected to one another is an internet (lower case i). The Internet is the biggest of all the internets. and consists of a worldwide collection of interconnected computer networks.

Internet Explorer One of the most popular pieces of browser software, produced by Microsoft.

Intranet A network of computers, which works in the same way as an internet, but for internal use, such as within a corporation.

ISDN/Integrated Services Digital Network Digital telephone line which facilitates very fast connections and can transfer larges amounts of data. It can carry more than one form of data at once.

ISP/Internet Service Provider See Access Provider.

Java Programming language which can be used to create interactive multimedia effects on webpages. The language is used to create programmes known as *applets* that add features such as animations, sound and even games to websites.

Javascript A scripting language which, like Java, can be used to add extra multimedia features. However, in contrast with Java it does not consist of separate programmes. Javascript is embedded into the HTML text and can interpreted by the browser, provided that the user has a javascript enabled browser.

JPEG Stands for 'Joint Photographic Experts Group' and is the name given to a type of format which compresses photos, so that they can be seen on the web.

Kill file A function which allows a user to block incoming information from unwanted sources.

Normally used on email and newsreaders.

LAN/Local Area Network A type of internet, but limited to a single area, such as an office.

Login The account name or password needed to access a computer system.

Link Connection between web pages, or one web document and another, which are accessed via formatted text and graphic.

Mailing List A discussion group which is associated with a website. Participants send their emails to the site, and it is copied and sent by the server to other individuals on the mailing list.

Modem A device for converting digital data into analogue signals for transmission along standard phone lines. The usual way for home users to connect to the internet or log into their email accounts. May be internal (built into the computer) or external (a desk-top box connected to the computer).

MP3 A compressed music file format, which has almost no loss of quality although the compression rate may be very high.

Netscape Popular browser, now owned by AOL.

Newbie Term for someone new to the Internet. Used perjoratively of newcomers to bulletin boards or chat, who commit the sin of asking obvious questions or failing to observe the netiquette.

Newsgroup Discussion group amongst Internet users who share an interest. There are thousands of newsgroups covering every possible subject.

Offline Not connected to the internet via a telephone line.

Online Connected to the internet via a telephone line.

Offline Browsing A function of the browser software, which allows the user to download pages and read them whilst offline.

Online Service Provider Similar to an access provider, but provides addtional features such as live chat.

PDF/Portable Document Format A file format created by Adobe for offline reading of brochures, reports and other documents with complex graphic design, which can be read by anyone with Acrobat Reader.

Plug-in Piece of software which adds more functions (such as playing music or video) to another, larger software program.

POP3/Post Office Protocol An email protocol that allows you to pick up your mail from any location on the web.

Portal A website which offers many services, such as search engines, email and chat rooms, and to which people are likely to return to often . ISPs such as Yahoo and Alta Vista provide portal sites which are the first thing you see when you log on, and in theory act as gateways to the rest of the web.

Post/Posting Information sent to a usenet group, bulletin board, message board or by email.

PPP/Point to Point Protocol The agreed way of sending data over dial-up connections, so that the user's computer, the modem and the Internet Server can all recognise it. It is the protocol which allows you to get online.

Protocol Convention detailing a set of actions that computers in a network must follow so that they can understand one another.

Query Request for specific information from a database.

RAM /Random Access Memory Your computer's short term memory.

Realplayer G2 A plug-in program that allows you to view video in real-time and listen to sound and which is becoming increasingly important for web use.

Router A computer program which acts as an interface between two networks, and decides how to route information.

Searchable Database A database on a website which allows the user to search for information, usually be keyword.

Search Engine Programs which enable web users to search for pages and sites using keywords. They are usually to be found on portal sites and browser homepages. Infoseek, Alta Vista and Lycos are some of the popular search engines.

Secure Transactions Information transfers which are encrypted so that only the sender and recipient have access to the uncoded message, so that the details within remain private. The term is most commonly used to refer to credit card transactions, although other information can be sent in a secure form.

Server A powerful computer that has a permanent fast connection to the internet. Such computers are usually owned by companies and act as host computers for websites.

Sign-on To connect to the internet and start using one of its facilities.

Shareware Software that doesn't have to be paid for or test version of software that the user can access for free, as a trial before buying it.

Skins Simple software that allows the user to change the appearance of an application.

Standard A style which the whole of the computer industry has agreed upon. Industry standards mean that hardware and software produced by the various different computer companies will work with one another.

Stream A technique for processing data, which enables it to be downloaded as a continuous stream, and viewed or listened to as the data arrives.

Surfing Slang for looking around the Internet, without any particular aim, following links from site to site.

TLA/Three Letter Acronyms Netspeak for the abbreviations of net jargon, such as BPS (Bits Per Second) and ISP (Internet Service Provider).

Upload To send files from your computer to another one on the internet. When you send an email you are uploading a file.

URL/Uniform Resource Locator Jargon for an address on the internet, such as www.thegoodwebguide.co.uk.

Usenet A network of newsgroups, which form a worldwide system, on which anyone can post 'news'.

Virtual Community Name given to a congregation of regular mailing list/ newsgroup users.

VRML/Virtual Reality Modeling Language Method for creating 3D environments on the web.

Wallpaper Description of the sometimes hectic background patterns which appear behind the text on some websites.

Web Based Email/Webmail Email accounts such as Hotmail and Rocketmail, which are accessed via an Internet browser, rather than an email program such as Outlook Express. Webmail has to be typed whilst the user is online, but can accessed from anywhere on the Web.

Webmaster A person responsible for a web server. May also be known as System Administrator.

Web Page Document which forms one part of a website (though some sites are a single page), usually formatted in HTML.

Web Ring Loose association of websites which are usually dedicated to the same subject and often contain links to one another.

Website A collection of related web pages which often belong to an individual or organisation and are about the same subject.

World Wide Web The part of the Internet which is easy to get around and see. The term is often mistakenly interchanged with Internet, though the two are not the same. If the Internet is a shopping mall, with shops, depots, and delivery bays, then the web is the actual shops which the customers see and use.

INDEX